/ 5 /

D0944231

Enjoy!

Fix Canada

Fourteenth Edition

Jeff Willerton

Copyright © 2000-2014 by Jeff Willerton
ISBN 978-0-9938835-0-7

PRINTED IN CANADA

Library and Archives Canada Cataloguing in Publication

Willerton, Jeff, 1964-

Fix Canada / by Jeff Willerton.

-- Fourteenth edition. Revised and Updated

Includes bibliographical references

ISBN 978-0-9938835-0-7

1. Canada -- Politics and government -- 1993-.
2. Alberta -- Politics and government -- 1971-.
3. Conservatism-- Canada. I. Title.

FC60.W45 2006   971.064'8   C2006-905082-1

Published in Canada by Emmanuel Publishing
a division of
Emmanuel Marketing Enterprises Ltd.
BOX 20008 East RPO
Airdrie, AB T4A 0C2

Cover Design by Patrick Glenn
Typesetting by Myron Achtman

To Dad, whose political zeal
had to rub off on someone:
I couldn't have asked for a
better example of how to do life.

Fix Canada

Who Is Saying What About This

"This is the flat-out best political book I've ever read, and I've read many."

Angie Warwick, School Trustee

"I don't do politics and have never read a political book in my life... until now. Wow!"

Jennifer Gardiner, Executive Administrative Assistant

"Willerton's words are infectious and refreshing, and I've read this collection of them four times – thus far!"

James Hansen, Stock Car Racer

"This is the only book I've ever read – five times!"

Ernie Boehm, Retired Chef

"The only other author I've read seven times is Tolkien."

Dmytro Kushneryk, Prep Cook

"I might disagree with half of what Willerton wrote here, but I don't care! I've never in my life read anything that stimulated so much intelligent political debate – and this book will be mandatory reading for my son one day."

John Telehanic, Sales

"The Mrs. and I are downsizing. She wanted to sell my books. 'Okay,' I said, 'but not this one. This one's for the grandkids.'"

Bob Timmins, Retiree

"I don't think I've ever read anything more insightful or entertaining, and there's also no small amount of truth between the covers of this book."

Bill Mann, Service Writer

"It's perfect the way Willerton put this together. A twelve year old or even a retired grease monkey like me could understand it."

James E. Bonsor, Retired Mechanic

"Willerton hits the bull's-eye in the middle of the bull's-eye... every time!"

Ben Hildebrandt, Businessman

"Willerton uses language the way it was intended to be used: well and to convey truth."

Tom Podollan, V.P. Operations

"I wasn't expecting much when I opened this book. Was I in for a surprise! Absolutely fantastic!"

Ritchie Johnston, Retired Consultant

"Little did I know when I bought this book that it would change the way I think on so many issues. What an eye-opener!"

Ted Hurlston, Retired Custodian

"If you really want to know what's happening in Canadian politics, you have to read this book. But you can't borrow mine. I'm not letting it out of my sight!"

Joleen Chouinard, to a friend, regarding the book you now hold.

"I'm 90 years old, and I didn't think I'd ever read a book like this. *It's about time someone wrote it!*"

W.V. (Wilf) Russell, Veteran

"The only disappointment in this book is that it ends. I could read Willerton forever."

Elsie Schmidt,
Administrative Assistant

Fix Canada

Table of Contents

Federal and International Issues:

Conclusion:

Introduction

Fix Canada

Introduction

This book comes about as the result of the death of a very fine man. John Moerman was a teenager in WWII Holland where he worked with the Dutch underground protecting downed Allied airmen. One day he had coffee with an SS officer at his kitchen table while hiding one such airman directly underneath. It's the stuff movies are made of!

After the war John married his sweetheart Corrie, they immigrating to the country of their liberators where they pastored churches in the Edmonton area for forty years. Retiring to a small acreage John became a prolific writer, articulately taking on the left-leaning establishment and defending those who could not do so themselves, a cause to which he often returned. As son Jack eulogized, his father fearlessly took on both Nazis and Canadian politicians alike!

His letters were sent regularly to over two hundred publications across Canada. When the editor of our local weekly needed a conservative columnist to complete his revised editorial page, the retired pastor heard the call. That is to say he heard the phone ring, accepted the offered promotion and became a very fine weekly columnist. Sadly, it would be his last paying gig. Six months later, without so much as a hint of either physical or mental decline, he was gone.

To understand how John affected the lives of the people he touched, one need only consider the example of the receptionist at the doctor's office where he had been taking his beloved Corrie before his passing. The two had been there about a dozen times. When informed of why a forthcoming appointment had to be cancelled, (his passing) she—the receptionist—simply exploded into tears right there in the office. Such was the effect he had on people who knew him even casually. I know; I was one.

It had been my privilege to meet John on three occasions. The first was in my role as a salesman in 1997. I introduced myself. He interjected: "Would that be the same Jeff Willerton who ran for Social Credit down in Calgary two weeks ago?" Note that there were probably 300 candidates across the province in that election, Alberta is three times the size of a unified Germany and I was a long way from home. Obviously this gentleman had a mind for details. He and Corrie and I coffeed away the balance of a very enjoyable afternoon.

The second time we met was at their 50th wedding anniversary into which I almost accidentally stumbled. I didn't particularly want to be back in their town that day but had been cornered by a business acquaintance into competing in a karaoke contest at a local hotel (that trophy now standing beside the monument to your then twelve year old author's budding skill on the chess board).

So it was a bit of happenstance that I was in their town that day, and a little bit more that I stopped to coffee with yet another acquaintance on the way out of it. He informed me of the festivities in town to which I informed him we simply had to go. Again a good time was had with the Moermans.

The third, two days later, was a brief encounter in which I gave John some literature he'd requested. It was brief but, as always, meaningful. He concluded it by looking me in the eye and saying, with a little twinkle in his own, "I think we think alike on a lot of issues." It was a meaningful encounter with a great man made more so by his sudden departure from the world five days later.

That departure left an ache in the heart of all who knew John Moerman... and a column-sized void on our editorial page. As I whispered to the newspaper God at the time, if it's offered to me I'll accept the responsibility and fill that space to the best of my ability. Forget offered; I finagled until I got it.

I'd been writing letters to the editor for some time, as had John before being elevated to the status of weekly columnist. His last words to me were, in effect, that we were of the same mind on many issues – a veritable passing of the mantle if you will.

In the beginning the space he had occupied became a guest column. Your humble scribe filled it for all but three weeks of the following six months, at which point the editor finally succumbed to mounting public pressure (... I'm public!) and gave it to me as my own byline. Much of what you hold in your hand is a compilation of those columns (edited, at times, for brevity and/or clarity) written over the year and a half following John's passing. As I wrote in the opening paragraph, this book comes about as the result of the death of a very fine man, and truer words would frankly be hard to find. I hope in this introduction to have in some small way honoured his memory.

The column was largely a critique of the liberal policies imposed on us by various levels of government. Left-leaning federales have done more than their share of damage to this country. Unfortunately the provinces have marched lock step with them to the edge of the abyss.

Ralph Klein, for instance, the country's then most supposedly conservative premier, spent money more liberally than any other provincial leader in the history of Confederation. He had it to spend you might argue, but so did Peter Lougheed, and it was Lougheed's unbridled spending that landed Alberta in the soup in the first place. Klein's enduring reputation as some kind of conservative hawk simply testifies to the efficacy of double-speak and smoke and mirror politics, as you will see.

Of course both he and Jean Chretien, another prominent figure in the book, have long since departed the political stage. So why read about them? Why did your humble scribe read a book about Lougheed in the summer of '06, twenty years after he left office? Or why would one ever read about Trudeau, or Napoleon? Because it's history, of course, and we all know what happens if we don't learn from it....

The columns were written as issues arose so to read them chronologically would be to bounce from one issue and jurisdiction to another and back again. To simplify, the book has been divided into two sections. The first deals primarily with provincial issues in Alberta, issues largely shared by other provinces. The author might have written a similar column in P.E.I., for instance, but it's probably a good thing this unfolded in Alberta as Ralph Klein cut a somewhat more national and obviously more colourful figure than Pat Binns. Who? Exactly! The second section deals with federal and international issues. An attempt was also made to gather issues together, when possible, without violating the above divisions.

Being somewhat controversial, obviously the column was not without its detractors. One memorable day a reader tore a strip off me for A) spilling too much ink on the provincial Tories [understandably, as he was a member of their local constituency association] and B) being overly negative.

To respond to the second accusation first, that of being overly negative, I confess my guilt: I was negative. One must add, though, that it's hard to put a positive spin on the political situation anywhere in Canada while being governed into the toilet. To do so in the late nineties when these columns were first penned would have lacked either journalistic integrity and/or a modicum of insight. Probably both.

In response to the accusation of spilling too much ink on the provincial Tories in Alberta: A) it was a political column, and B) I live in the province. Naturally one would focus his writings on the politics of the jurisdiction in which he resides. Lastly, and in the words of another reader, "They deserved every drop!"

And so they did. They're far from alone, of course, but if the most notably conservative government in Canada is as liberal, and therefore duplicitous, as revealed in these pages, we obviously have a lot of rooting out to do. And not only provincially....

The federal Liberals and the pre-merger Progressive Conservative Party of Canada (historically) have been almost equally culpable for our nation's decline, if not completely indistinguishable. They've been aptly compared to two vehicles splashing each other with mud, travelling on the same road, in the same direction, to the exact same destination.

The players were well aware of this and seemingly entirely comfortable under either banner: Tory cabinet minister Jean Charest served as the Liberal premier of Quebec for three terms; admitted Trudeau fan and lifelong card-carrying Liberal Ralph Klein served as the Conservative premier of Alberta for almost fourteen years; and one-time Conservative Prime Minister Joe Clark was seen campaigning for Benedict Arnold (aka: Scott Brison) in Nova Scotia in 2004. If you, like me, are a victim of the public education system and thus presumably unfamiliar with the name, Benedict Arnold was BFF with George Washington and a general in the revolutionary army before defecting to the British. If you're over seventy and unfamiliar with the acronym, BFF stands for 'best friends forever', the closeness of their relationship making the defection that much more egregious.

North of the 49th, many Canadians seem determined to vote as they and their families have for the last hundred years, apparently more concerned with maintaining tradition than seeking good governance. I'm referring now, post merger and the creation of the Conservative Party of Canada, to those who persist in voting Liberal despite 'da proof' that they're thieves and finance their election campaigns with that stolen loot; or for the marginally further left NDP which has thus far managed to cripple the potential of the provinces in which it has governed; or, where they continue to exist, for the Progressive (meaning liberal, thus conflicted) Conservatives.

Many Albertans, for instance, will likewise go to the polls and vote Tory again, A) because they always have, or B) because that party temporarily balanced the budget and paid off the debt. Of course those who base their vote on tradition have limited grounds on which to criticize others who do the same, (like federal Liberal supporters, for instance) and those who base their vote on the Tories' financial record overlook the fact that anyone who couldn't do at least what that gang did in this resource-rich province, in that era, should probably be institutionalized. I am, though, starting to pilfer from the column.

Speaking of which it was a privilege to write it. I have no formal training as a writer nor in the subject matter contained herein. I'm just a high school educated political layman with a passion for promoting better government. To do so, obviously it would help to know a little bit about the subject.

To that end you might say I've built a sort of grid of information over the years through which new information and events are filtered. To the extent the grid is faulty, so too will be said interpretations. Likewise to the extent the grid is properly built. You will be the judge as to its construction.

I don't profess to have plumbed any issue to its depths. I might believe I have a somewhat broad understanding of political issues. You might agree, adding that it's pretty shallow. Or not, but what will your judgment be based on, of course, if not your grid?

To understand the early columns one must be made aware of what were then some recent developments in the province. One was the Supreme Court's Vriend decision in which the high court agreed with an Alberta Court of Queen's Bench ruling to read 'sexual orientation' into the province's Individual Rights legislation. Another was that over the previous years the Tory government had brought electronic gambling devices known as Video Lottery Terminals into the province and placed them pretty much anywhere a person could sit down for a cold one.

Vriend, VLTs, judge-made law, major political cover ups and many other issues are dealt with in these pages. Occasionally some good news even creeps in. Depending on one's particular paradigm, or world view, one might find points with which one agrees and others with which one will perhaps even strongly disagree. Hopefully more of the former than the latter.

Should the column itself, though, have been written? It was well received by the readership, so probably, yes. But what of the book? More to the point, should it have been honed and redesigned these several times now as I approach the publication of this fourteenth and (keeping in mind that I've said this nine times now) presumably final edition? In fact I was almost daily asking myself a similar question in the spring of '07 for reasons that will later be made clear. The answer came while reading a book on 18th century philosopher Adam Smith.

Smith is widely revered as the Father of Capitalism for his work, *Wealth of the Nations* (1776). This much I knew. What I discovered therein was that *Wealth* was almost an addendum to his earlier, seminal work entitled *The Theory of Moral Sentiments*. This he first published in 1759 – and republished, "honed and re-designed"[1] five times in the thirty-one years following.

Hold the phone(!) and note the timing. Questioning if I was on the right road publishing and republishing a book to a significant extent about social issues, (known in an earlier era as 'moral sentiments') it came to my attention that the one I was on had been trod before by no less than the Father of Capitalism himself! The moment was surreal! After it there was simply no question about continuing with this project. Not everyone will share my enthusiasm.

Comparing the home of the brave with our native land, one McGill University economist surmised: "You can be a social conservative in the U.S. without being labelled a whacko. Not in Canada." If this is true, some will be tempted to write me off in short order.

I believe, for instance, that it is wrong for society to grant marriage licences to gay couples or otherwise endorse or further normalize a lifestyle that is widely known to slay its adherents in their prime and contributes frankly nothing to that society beyond, perhaps, the very temporal emotional comfort of those adherents.

In view of today's zeitgeist (a German word meaning 'spirit of the age') it is understood that the preceding borderline run-on sentence will inevitably alienate more than a few readers, and not only for its structure. It is hoped, though, that even those in deepest disagreement will also be gracious enough to read on and discover the relative logic behind it and other positions articulated between these covers.

I likewise believe, for instance, that it's wrong for governments to place what is known as the crack cocaine of gambling devices under people's noses in bars and restaurants across the land. Like John Moerman before me, I also do my editorial best to defend those yet incapable of doing so themselves.

One is of course free to disagree with any or all of these positions. Unfortunately for those who do, those issues (gay rights, VLTs and abortion) are the first three dealt with in the book you're presently reading and comprise the first approximately dozen columns. And then like a dog with a bone buried in the back yard, I occasionally return to them.

Winston Churchill defined a fanatic as "one who can't change his mind and won't change the subject." Again, you will be the judge as to whether I qualify.

I by no means have the final word on the issues contained herein, but humbly submit my thoughts on them to you for your consideration. They may enrich or enrage you—or both—but I have a sneaking suspicion they won't leave you entirely unmoved. Enjoy!

Fix Canada

Provincial Issues

Orientation a choice?

April 20,1998

Many will disagree with this statement, but I maintain that sexual orientation is—at least likely—a choice. What can be said definitively is that there is no empirical evidence to support the theory that people are born gay, and that the circumstantial evidence, if one cares to give it even a passing glance, strongly indicates otherwise.

Consider, for example, the innumerable instances of genetically identical twins in which one embraces the gay lifestyle and the other not. If they were born that way, as the argument goes, wouldn't they both be gay? Perhaps I'm just not worldly enough, but it seems to me there must be something else going on here.

Consider also the hypothetical example of identical twin boys separated at birth: one raised by a heterosexual couple; the other by two gay men. Ask yourself honestly: which child do you think will be more inclined to experiment with the homosexual lifestyle? It's a rhetorical question. That environment influences development is a long established fact.

This having been said, I'm not 'anti-gay' and the backlash in Alberta against the Supreme Court's Vriend decision (reading sexual orientation into the province's human rights legislation) is not tantamount to hostility toward the homosexual community. Most people, your scribe included, have a live-and-let-live mentality. They have no desire to go back to the days when people were thrown in jail for being gay, (clearly that was an excess) but nor, I suspect, do they want them given carte blanche to mold our youth in the school system or anywhere else for that matter. People need to be free to live their lives as they choose without fear of being bullied obviously, but so too others need to be free to protect their loved ones from exposure to the promotion of what they deem an enormously destructive lifestyle.

And by no means should anyone be put at ease today by Premier Ralph Klein's repeated assertions that 'fences' will be put up around the areas of fostering and adoption. Not many months ago the same Ralph Klein was specifically musing about permitting the same, so his opposition to it now seems a tad contrived, not that it matters. In reality the fences will be built; they will be challenged; they will be torn down. After Vriend it'll be child's play for the gay lobby.

Governments are tasked with the job of creating, to the best of their ability, environments in which it is safe to live, work and do business. I repeat – 'safe-to-live'. To either promote or allow the promotion of a lifestyle widely known to slay its adherents in their prime is entirely antithetical to that mandate.

UPDATE: Note that no legislative attempt was ever made to build the aforementioned fences, and shortly after making those fallacious promises the government of Alberta began actively approving both gay and lesbian applications for fostering and adoption. As a result, a lawyer specializing in the same estimated that between 2000 and 2005 over two hundred children had been adopted by gay couples in the province.

Now whether or not it's healthy for baby Levon to be raised by Elton John and his Canadian partner, David Furnish, for instance, would make for lively debate. Unfortunately legislation with the potential to rob the author of his free-speech right to question that familial arrangement came into effect in 2004. It began as a private member's bill put forth by none other than openly gay jewel thief and former B.C. NDP Member of Parliament, Svend Robinson.

On the issue of Svend's life of crime, (recall that he was surveilled pocketing a very expensive engagement ring) note that without gay marriage, of which he was an early and staunch proponent, there would have been no engagement plans and no stolen ring. And he'd probably still be an MP! It's poetic irony. He tearily blamed his light fingers on depression. Believe it or not, grandchildren, once upon a time, 'gay' meant 'happy'. Don't laugh at your grandfather. I'm serious!

'Marriage' doesn't quite mean what it used to, either. Adam and Eve can still get married, but so can Svend and Max since gay marriage became the law of the land in July, 2005. Note that the same Pierre Trudeau who gave us *The Charter of Rights and Freedoms* (1982) that led to this point specifically promised no less than seven times prior to its passage that it would not do so. One can't know that he was consciously misleading us, of course, but if gay marriage can be shown to be detrimental to western society, and he to have subscribed to a philosophy hell-bent on its downfall, then obviously the possibility looms large.

A confidante of Castro and an open admirer of Mao, a woman Trudeau went to university with maintains he was then a proud card-carrying communist. According to an internal 1968 RCMP report, (trumpeted by a retired officer stumping for political office) our then future prime minister also had the distinction of leading a delegation of communists to the 1952 Moscow Economic Forum.

Not convinced? In his own words: "(B)etween the years 1952 and 1960 I was several times forbidden to teach in the universities... because of my anticlerical *and communist leanings"* (Pierre Elliot Trudeau, *Federalism and the French Canadians,* St. Martin's Press, 1968, p. xxi, emphasis added). In the same book he claimed that "the very purpose of a collective system is (to) better ensure personal freedom" (p. 209) and that NDP style "democratic socialism may be less efficient than the totalitarian brand" (p. 150). So the evidence for Trudeau's communism is overwhelming, (I've barely scratched the surface here) and the communist objective to undermine the west has never exactly been a well kept secret.

In light of these observations, even the most blinkered Liberal must concede the possibility that Trudeau's signature achievement, the Charter, was never the benevolent document that was sold to us but rather a Trojan Horse from which continues to creep sundry enemies of the state. Like gay marriage. Allow me to explain.

In 1927, Stalin published his agenda for the west which included the advocation of "companionate marriage."[2] Shack-ups. Why? To "destroy the bonds of domestic life... *by doing away with marriage"*[3] (emphasis added). One way to destroy a venerable institution like marriage would be to remove all meaning from it, thus explaining what the author believes has been the very intentional watering down of the definition of matrimony in the west these past forty years.

Why, though, would communists (assuming Trudeau was one and wasn't acting completely independently) promote homosexuality abroad while continuing to ban even the tacit promotion of it today in their own country? (Remember Sochi?) To promote the demise of western civilization, and the preservation of their own, is frankly the only explanation that makes a lick of sense. More to follow....

Tolerate this!

January 25, 1999

To "tolerate," according to Webster, is "to allow without hindrance; (to) permit; (or) endure." Its noun form, 'tolerance', is taught in many schools today as the quintessential virtue, all others, like chivalry, bravery, honesty and courtesy, being dwarfed by it. Leslie Armour, a philosophy professor at the University of Ottawa, contends that "to be a virtuous citizen is to be one who tolerates everything except intolerance." The apparent contradiction could be lost on this PhD. (To wit: it's intolerant to be intolerant of intolerance.)

Today's tolerance bears little resemblance to its original meaning. Today it means more than to simply 'permit' or 'endure', but to actively embrace and hold as true even those claims which conflict with one's own. It's also, of course, complete rubbish.

The Law of Non-Contradiction insists that two contradictory ideas cannot both be true. They might both be false, but they can't possibly both be true. Proponents of today's 'tolerance' seem blind to this simple fact.

Some maintain, for instance, that homosexuality is innate, or inborn. I do not. Obviously someone is wrong. There are, it can be safely assumed, both intra and post-uterine influences that can affect one's sexual preferences. A domineering mother; an MIA father; a history of abuse; influence of peers... obviously there are myriad possible predisposing factors, but note: none of them unequivocally dictate behaviour.

That people in that lifestyle have made what I consider to be poor choices along the way (like to experiment with homosexuality in the first place) gives me no license to persecute or judge them, and I don't. I make poor choices – different, but nonetheless poor.

So I have no right to judge them, nor do I, but nor do I condone their behavior. I tolerate it according to the dictionary definition of the word, but I cannot condone or endorse it. Nor should I.

Condoning what I know to be one of the most dangerous lifestyles on earth would be akin to applauding my brother's trek across a fast moving river on thin ice. As his keeper it would behoove me to try to stop him from beginning the trip and, failing that, to do all in my power to help him off the ice. Anything less, frankly, would be negligent.

UPDATE: The present zeitgeist dictates that people are born gay, much like being born black or white, and that gay marriage is about treating people equally. Wrong and... well, bad policy anyway.

First of all, if homosexuality is genetic its prevalence would not be dictated by either period or locale, but in reality in some epochs it's been almost obligatory (the Greco-Roman era, for instance) and in others almost entirely unheard of. (Think rural Kansas, circa 1850.) There may well be other factors at play, but one can assume from this that the prevalence of homosexuality in society is at least partially a cultural issue.

The argument that gay marriage is about treating people equally is also deeply flawed. Prior to 07/05 I couldn't marry Jimmy and neither could Steve, but any one of the three of us could have married Sue if she were willing. So we were equal, and, importantly, we were treated equally for equal behaviour. What gay marriage is really about is treating different things equally, which, according to Chesterton, (1874-1936) is itself the very height of inequality. If I didn't know better I'd think the man was ahead of his time.

One 'Conservative' who isn't.

April 04, 1999

I have little but contempt for the provincial Tories in Alberta. In '71 they took over a province run on a pay-as-you-go basis and drove it into debtors' prison. What was one of the country's richest provinces was eventually saddled with one of its largest per capita debts.

In '92 Ralph Klein rode in on a white steed and single-handedly reversed the situation if you believe his many admirers. In reality a stoned monkey might have done every bit as good a job of it with the resource revenues we've experienced, but I won't belabour the issue. The books were balanced and the debt substantially chipped away at during his tenure, all very true. Some believe this makes Ralph a good conservative. With all due respect, they couldn't be more wrong.

One's fiscal decisions are irrevocably correlated to one's social convictions. If a socialist, for instance, is committed to providing an equal outcome for all regardless of individual effort or ability, and has control of the levers of the economy, certain economic decisions naturally follow and all are eventually left equally poor.

On the other side of the spectrum, a pure libertarian who believes in individual liberty and responsibility would let those who will, starve to death. Most people fall somewhere between these two extremes, (like Liberals and Conservatives) but my point is that people's philosophical and social beliefs ultimately determine their fiscal priorities.

I maintain, therefore, that people cannot be both socially liberal and fiscally conservative at the same time. Thus if Mr. Klein appears to be both, assuming I'm correct, one must be a facade. At a March caucus meeting this year he made it painfully clear which it is.

Conservatives are called such because they conserve; Liberals change stuff. Or at least that's the way it's supposed to work, but to quote Neil Waugh of the *Edmonton Sun,* our so-called conservative government (at the above noted meeting) "has unleashed forces that will reshape our world and see same-sex foster families, adoption and marriage in everything but name (called 'registered domestic partnerships') an Alberta reality."

Likewise family benefits for homosexuals. Such were created because of what families contribute to society – specifically the next generation of citizens. Giving people the freedom to live their lives as they choose is defensible to a point. Subsidizing their societally destructive choices is another matter entirely.

ADDENDUM: If people are born gay, obviously they can't be held responsible for having chosen that lifestyle. On p. 37 the author states (again) that there is no empirical evidence to support that theory. Critics will argue there is much, but the reality is that minute differences between the brains of heterosexuals and homosexuals, which they inevitably point to, prove nothing. Do these changes lead to homosexuality or does homosexuality lead to these changes? In fact we don't know, but what is widely known is that behaviour, particularly repetitive behaviour, influences neural development strongly indicating the latter. Life is about choices. The reasons people make those choices are manifold and complex, granted, but to suggest that the decisions thusly arrived at are genetically determined is not supported by either science or common sense.

Klein + Truth
=
Cannot Compute!

June 07, 1999

The Supreme Court recently redefined 'spouse' as anyone you want it to be, regardless of gender. In the Ontario case known as M vs. H, one lesbian was suing another for what she deemed to be the fair disbursement of business and personal assets because they slept together. The lower court insisted on maintaining the definition of spouse as someone of the opposite sex.

The Supremes in an 8 to 1 ruling decided this was discriminatory according to the Charter and struck down said definition. Soon there will be no way to legally discriminate against a same sex couple who want to apply for a marriage license anywhere in Canada.

"Hallelujah!" cried B.C. Premier Glen Clark. Well, almost. What he did say was that this decision was "very good news" and that "it's time we treated people with equity and dignity regardless of their sexual orientation." At least he's honest about his support for the ruling.

Ralph Klein is anything but: "I don't know if we're ready to go in that direction," he muttered, ever wary of his need to appeal to Martha and Henry, his fictitious, severely normal, conservative Albertans.

This, of course, is from the same guy who only two months earlier promoted homosexual 'rights' to foster and adopt kids while dallying with the concept of 'registered domestic partnerships' which, if implemented, would make state sanctioned homosexual unions an Alberta reality.

'Registered domestic partnership', he assured us, is a civil term – marriage a religious one. Not so fast, Mr. In fact people are every bit as 'married' by justices of the peace as they are by ministers of the gospel, so marriage is very much a civil term.

Thus whether two people are joined in holy matrimony in a church or legally married by a representative of the state is irrelevant insofar as family benefits are concerned. They both qualify, as soon will those in Alberta's registered domestic partnerships.

Now open-minded though I may be, I am nevertheless convinced that it is self-evidently lacking in wisdom to subsidize a lifestyle that's killing people around the world. We can accept people for who they are, where they are, without rewarding destructive behaviour. To do so would be to encourage more of the same, and if you'll follow the bouncing ball for a moment, more homosexuality ipso facto leads to less heterosexuality, lower levels of reproduction and, taken to its logical conclusion, societal demise. Am I suggesting that widespread homosexuality poses an existential threat to society? A very gay latter-day Roman Empire arguably collapsed from within. Assuming that a correlation exists between these facts, what exactly makes you think we're immune?

UPDATE: The unstated assumption made in these pages is that there is a correlation between the defining act of the homosexual lifestyle—anal sex—and the proliferation of AIDS. In fact the World Health Organization essentially conceded this point in 2008 when it admitted that the long predicted AIDS pandemic will not be for the simple reason that the disease is largely contained within high risk groups, most prominently, particularly in developed countries, the male homosexual community. This is entirely logical.

Firstly, consider that AIDS is a blood borne disease. Because of the structural difference between columnar (side by side) and epithelial (layered) cells, there is also reportedly three times as much microscopic bleeding in anal as opposed to vaginal sex. Add these together and the high rate of AIDS in the homosexual community becomes at the same time both a regrettable but easily understood development.

If people aren't preprogrammed to be gay, (the premise of these first columns) how do they become so? Predisposing factors notwithstanding, I believe people almost invariably do so through the three step process of confusion, experimentation and addiction.

Young people are confused about a lot of things today including, in increasingly higher numbers in our gay promoting culture, their sexual identities. These are encouraged by others farther down that road to experiment with the lifestyle and find that, much like the rest of humanity, they respond to human touch. Repeated experiences leading to pleasurable results create patterns and increasingly entrenched habits.

Men, then, become addicted to the easy orgasm (male sex partners are easy to find if one knows where to look and, unlike women, aren't notably discriminating); women to plastic, with which flesh and blood cannot compete. At many points along the way the message is driven home that 1) they were born that way, and 2) they cannot change. The first claim is unsupported by empirical evidence; the second is a brazen lie.

As the 1994 study The Social Organization of Sexuality [4] makes clear, the vast majority of those who succumb to the pull of homosexuality eventually do leave the lifestyle, so it can be done. If this is an issue for the reader, the writer strongly encourages a visit to www.PeopleCanChange.com. To another issue....

VLTs must go

May 11, 1998

The esteemed writer in the space above this one argued last week that people need to be as free to plug their loonies into Video Lottery Terminals as they are to buy cigarettes or liquor or to participate in any other form of self-destructive behaviour. What my libertarian colleague failed to note is that our freedoms are daily curtailed in the interests of promoting the greater public good, and sometimes need to be.

One is not free to race down the highway at 200 km/hr. At any speed one is forced by law to wear a seat belt. I still struggle with this last one but know that it exists for both my well being and that of the public that finances the medical system. Ditto for motorcycle helmets. Most people have little trouble accepting such reasonable limitations for the good of society.

One difference between VLTs and other vices like smoking and drinking is that governments actively discourage the latter through significant levels of taxation while at the same time promoting the former. The Tories brought VLTs into the province, and by placing them just about everywhere a person can sit down for a cold one they've promoted them about as much as they can without actually running an ad.

My aforementioned colleague goes on to state that he has never personally met anyone who has lost their house, car, spouse or kids because of their gambling habits. Sadly I've met a number, and I predict my sheltered friend will too, sooner rather than later. Apparently their numbers are on the rise.

Or so one can easily assume after the revelation that the Tories are sitting on a report detailing the number of problem gamblers in the province while spouting a figure gleaned from a pre '93, pre VLT study. If that percentage were decreasing it would be front page news, but as it's obviously increasing since the introduction of these bandits the government wants to (get this) 'study' the report until after the plebiscite on their future this fall. This willingness to withhold valuable information from the voting public is indicative of a government that will go to any lengths to manipulate the outcome of any so-called process of consultation.

If the duplicitous and deceptive Tories want to keep VLTs in the province, that alone is reason enough for me to vote against them. Cocaine and LSD long ago became banned substances for the greater public good, and few indeed beyond the junkies themselves argue for their return. So too VLTs should be shown the door, at least of the bars and restaurants.

UPDATE: Under a good deal of public pressure the Tories released the figures of the above mentioned study in the summer of '98. The number of problem gamblers in the province had gone from 39,000 to 72,000, an 85% increase according to most calculators. The government's press release reported this as a .6% increase, and the lamestream media dutifully reported it as such without so much as a word of explanation. In fact the increase amounts to, yes, .6% – of the entire population of Alberta! According to that logic, if the number of problem gamblers in the province had jumped from, say, ten, to 1.7 million, for instance, we'd still be looking at only a 50% increase. Apparently there's a spin doctor in Ralph's stable of three hundred (I'm not exaggerating) who earned his keep that day.

They call it 'Gaming'

June 28, 1999

'Gambling' has somewhat of a stigma attached to it, so some bright light euphemistically renamed it 'gaming'. Regardless of what it's called, it's merely a way to suck money out of people who have what are almost invariably false hopes of making it big. With rare exception the only ones who do are those organizing the affair, be it government, industry or Mafioso.

It's also spreading like wildfire in many nations in the world destroying marriages, undermining the work ethic, increasing crime, motivating suicide and destroying the financial security of untold numbers of families. This column is motivated by the recent news of a man who took a hatchet to five VLTs in an Edmonton city bar.

Over the previous two years he'd lost about $20,000 in the money-sucking vacuums. Now odds are this gentleman isn't a Rhodes scholar, but the fact is anyone is capable of becoming addicted to most any form of gambling. That said, most gambling addicts have less education and lower incomes than the general population, and it is they on whom the purveyors of this vice depend. Fully fifty percent of lottery tickets, for example, are purchased by only ten percent of the buyers – the vast majority of whom can be described as fitting into the aforementioned categories. In light of this, is it not safe to conclude that our governments are guilty of shamelessly exploiting the poor and uneducated?

In New Brunswick, an East Indian convenience store owner was sick of watching the welfare moms in her community flush their cheques down the toilet in her store's VLT while their kids went without basics. She phoned the government and asked them to remove the machine. They refused.

She then organized other convenience store owners in the province and phoned again. Still nothing, so she gave them seven days to get all the machines out or they'd be on the streets. Seven days later the streets of New Brunswick were littered with VLTs and the government was forced to pick them up.

That woman is a hero and I'm sorry there aren't more Canadians like her who will forego personal revenues in light of the social chaos created by these machines. Alberta's bar owners alternatively fight tooth and nail to hang on to their cash cows regardless of their broader social implications. Or rather, most of our bar owners.

Sid Ghotme owns a couple of watering holes in Calgary. He saw what VLTs did to the atmosphere in his establishments—to say nothing of the individual lives of his patrons—and he chucked them. And years later he's still doing a booming business, so don't tell me bar owners can't wean themselves off that revenue.

The province's most shameless gambling addict says he won't throw taxpayer cash at professional hockey teams. That's good, but regarding that issue Klein adds he's "looking at a number of options, including a sports lottery." Poor and uneducated be warned.

UPDATE: Alberta's various gambling devices (VLTs, slots and lotteries) brought in $864 million in 1999. Not satisfied, the government was in 2000 considering lifting the cap of 6,000 machines in the province despite promises made during the VLT debate only two years earlier that the cap would remain. Not co-incidentally, calls to Gamblers Anonymous went from 120 in 1992 (the year VLTs were introduced to the province) to 2,700 in 1999, a 2200% increase assum-ing you're not a Tory spin doctor. Do you think the Tories didn't understand that dramatically increasing the opportunities to gamble would likewise increase the number of addicts in the province? The opposite, of course, is also true.

In 1999, a South Carolina woman sat mesmerized in front of a VLT while her baby died of dehydration in the back of her sweltering car. The state responded by banning the machines. What is noteworthy, according to a CBC news documentary, is that calls to the local Gamblers Anonymous hotline then fell as precipitously as they had risen following their introduction.

In early '09 a scantily clad twenty-one month old tot was found in a car outside a Calgary casino in subzero temperatures while dad got his fix (an apparently not uncommon baby-sitting technique among addicts). State response: nada. Why? That's obvious: money.

When the government was contemplating bringing VLTs into the province, naturally it engaged in consul-tations with experts in the field. According to people who were privy to those meetings, the Tories were informed that they would enjoy a bonanza of wealth for fifteen years, followed by a dramatic spike in the social costs related to these blood-sucking machines. It would appear that they opted for short-term gain.

Governments are tasked, if you recall, with creating an environment in which it is 'safe to live, work and do business'. I repeat, again, for emphasis, 'safe-to-live'. Between rolling over on gay marriage and the outright promotion of gambling addictions, it appears the Al-berta Tories have other priorities.

There 'are' ramifications, you know

November 30, 1998

The year is 2010, and I'm a twenty-two year old male with AIDS. Twelve years ago in 1998 I was a healthy, energetic ten year old lad with a bright future. Unfortunately that was also the year then Premier Ralph Klein accepted the Supreme Court of Canada's decision to read 'sexual orientation' into the province's Individual Rights Act.

The public schools jumped in with both feet naturally, but soon even the various religious communities couldn't prevent homosexual activists from propagating their beliefs in their children's sex-ed classes. Being of tender age and largely uninformed about sexual issues, yours truly bought into the lie that theirs was a safe alternative lifestyle. If it were, of course, I wouldn't be writing this today.

Don't get me wrong: I accept full responsibility for my role in my own demise, but I wasn't the only actor in this play, you understand. A fellow named Trudeau wrote the script, called *The Charter.* His appointed Supreme Court judges dutifully played their parts, and the premier/protagonist mentioned above played the role of a double agent. That is to say he fought the case all the way to the Supreme Court only to then turn around and defend their decision, all on the taxpayers' dime, and in both cases his performance was simply flawless!

Now you will recall that at ten I was somewhat confused about sexual issues. Apparently I wasn't alone. A 1992 Minnesota Adolescent Health Survey of over 34,000 students found that 25.9% of twelve year olds were uncertain as to whether they were hetero or homosexual, whereas only 5% of seventeen year olds expressed similar confusion. And therein, I believe, lay the gay lobby's motivation to reach out to me, metaphorically speaking, in the classroom that day: I was impressionable.

The year is 1998 and you will realize the above account is futuristic and fictional, but not very. As sure as the sun will rise and set tomorrow, it's plain that there will be a fallout from these Tory policies. The Conservatives destroyed this province fiscally during the '70s and '80s through the inept mismanagement of our resources, and now they're doing it to us socially through these and other policies. They need to be beaten and, like the above scenario, said beating is not only possible but inevitable... I think. Stay tuned.

UPDATE: It's possible to beat the Tories in Alberta, but one might have added in '98 that it's going to take a while. Sixteen years later I've run against them six times under a number of different banners beginning with the old Social Credit Party in '97. I was still hanging around with that group when these columns were written, so naturally you will read an endorsement of them here from time to time, as in the following column. More on this shortly.

It can be done

December 7, 1998

In last week's column I presented some obvious and very negative consequences of the Alberta Tories' policies, particularly their endorsement of the Vriend decision. I also indicated that they needed to be beaten, and that said beating was possible.

It is, but they can't be beaten by the left – because they are the left! As if to make my case a number of federal Liberal supporters have suggested to your scribe that they're very content with that party's brand of... 'conservatism'. Thus I conclude that if the Tories are going to be beaten they have to be sacked from the right and shown up as the liberals they are, and the only party in a position to do that, in this province today, is Social Credit. Albertans, though, will have to break with tradition to bring back a party they once ousted.

The Liberals, for instance, were given the boot sixteen years after being installed by their federal counterpart when we joined Confederation in 1905, never to be returned to office again. (Let us pray.) The United Farmers of Alberta governed from 1921 to '35 when Social Credit was swept to power. The Socreds governed for thirty-six years and are remembered by many as the best government this province ever had.

The Tories took the reigns in '71, a year that marked the beginning of what I call the Dark Ages of Alberta politics. The so-called Conservatives nearly bankrupted the richest province in the country during their first twenty years in office, in part by creating the largest per capita bureaucracy in one of the most over-governed countries on earth. Today they're focusing their attention on undermining our social fabric and frankly deserve little but the contempt of the voting public for their efforts.

As one-time Deputy Premier Ken Kowalski once said regarding the future of his party, "All good things must come to an end." Yes and thankfully, according to commonly accepted wisdom, bad things do too.

UPDATE: The 2007 Financial Investment Planning and Advisory Commission advised that the province was facing a $215 Billion unfunded liability twenty years hence, and—news flash—neither Ed Stelmach, Alison Redford nor Jim Prentice created that problem. It was inherited lock, stock and barrel from their predecessors who were obviously rotten money managers, and one of the purposes of this book has been to show the need for more legitimately conservative government in Alberta. But which party?

The right in the province was getting a little crowded in '07, what with the Alberta Party, the Alberta Alliance and, new that year, the Wildrose Party. (The Socreds no longer qualify as they're all over the map.) It got a little less so in early '08 with the merger of the latter two under the Wildrose Alliance banner, the objective of all being the defeat of the Tories, naturally.

People say it can't be done. Of course they once said the same thing about the federal Liberals, but then along came a merger and a little thing called Adscam, and by June of 2004 defeat was staring that government in the face. A Conservative victory was possible—a majority even plausible—until with only ten days left to go in the campaign Ralph Klein rode to then Prime Minister Paul Martin's rescue with a knife to stab Stephen Harper in the back.

You will recall Ralph's proposed health care reforms which were to challenge "some people's interpretations of the Canada Health Act." His 'reforms' turned out to be no more than a simple tax increase that never materialized, but Klein's public musings gave Paul Martin the opportunity to make the groundless claim that he and Harper were colluding to do an end run around the Canada Health Act. With friends like that, of course, Stephen Harper had little need for enemies.

Five months later Klein had to face the Alberta electorate and needed to put some distance between himself and the gun control/gay marriage/Kyoto supporting government he helped re-elect. That's when the health care summit became a "Gong Show" and he took off after the first day to drop a G note in the slots in Hull.

What Ralph does with his money is entirely his business, of course, but it should be noted that those thousand bones were among the many he is paid to defend Albertans' other monies. Notably, it was during his absence that substantial increases to provincial transfers were announced. It is well known that as Canada's largest per capita benefactor such increases substantially hurt, rather than help, Alberta's bottom line.

Klein talked right up 'till the end of his career about standing up to Ottawa and defending Alberta's interests, but what did he say in 2005? "10.9 billion, (ripped out of the province) that's good, with an escalator, whatever that may be. That's good, too." That 10.9 billion 'escalated' to twenty one billion dollars in 2009. As one senior Alberta Member of Parliament put it, "Ralph cut a bad deal... so live with it." For those who continue to think he was the best thing since sliced bread, Ritalin is the prescribed intervention.

No funding, fewer abortions

May 18, 1998

We have a Young Offenders Act in this country because as a society we wouldn't want to execute ten year olds were we to bring back the ultimate deterrent. Some argue for the Act's repeal. Although changes may be necessary, (for nothing is perfect, let alone the YOA) the need for its continued existence in some form or other virtually goes without saying. This column is not about the YOA.

I take no pleasure in broaching the subject, but while we protect some of our nation's children through vehicles like the Young Offenders Act, others are burned with saline, dismembered without the benefit of an anesthetic or are otherwise destroyed through tax-funded abortions. The tax-funded issue I may return to another day, but for now I give the government their due under the laws of the current regime. What they do with it is their responsibility and perhaps they'll have to answer for it one day. The issues that need to be addressed here are those of the practice itself and that of constitutional protection.

Consider, for instance, the dichotomy of 'almost' new-born twins. The elder 'born' twin has full protection, while it continues to be open season on the younger yet passing through the birth canal. Is that fair, or just (as in 'just society') considering that the only actual difference between them is mere seconds of completely normal development?

When should constitutional protection for the child in the womb begin? Geneticists and biologists agree that we are what we are at conception. A person's height, eye colour, body type, intellect, (to a degree) etc.... all these are determined when the sperm hits the egg. Everything thereafter is simply development.

Now I ask you: does the walking child have more intrinsic value than the crawling child? The former is more developed than the latter, but the answer is clearly 'no'. Do you have any more intrinsic value than you had ten years ago? Of course not! You might be a little wiser with the passage of time, but your intrinsic value as a human being is not based on your development or maturity but on the simple fact of your being. Cannot the same logic apply equally to the child in the womb? Of course it can, but this is an issue, like many others, into which logic will always be an unwelcome intruder.

UPDATE: Why do the unborn have no rights in this country? Blame rests largely on abortion rights activist Dr. Henry Morgentaler, but he didn't act alone. He was aided and abetted in his fight for liberalized abortion laws in this country primarily by two women, Carolyn Egan and Cheri McDonald, both then members of a communist front known as the International Socialist.

Note that in Stalin's previously reported agenda for the west he also promoted "the advocation of legalized abortion."[5] Adding these seemingly disparate facts together, one cannot help but note the possibility that Morgentaler was simply a pawn in a long, deadly game, ultimately won by the Kremlin. And if that's the case, and you are among the reportedly 46% of Canadians comfortable with today's tax-funded, abortion-on-demand status quo in this country, sorry to inform, but you're philosophically in bed with a mass murderer. And I don't mean Henry Morgentaler.

Abortions not reduced by murder

November 02, 1998

The end NEVER, EVER justifies the means. Men like Lenin and Stalin didn't understand this simple truth. To them, liquidating 20,000,000 people was an acceptable sacrifice if it promoted the ultimate welfare of future generations in their communist utopia. Most, I hope, realize that the end they sought was just as messed as the means they used to arrive there.

Apparently the sniper who killed abortionist Dr. Barnett Slepian in New York two weeks ago is subject to the same ends/means folly. If this individual's purpose was to promote his cause (we presume, life) his actions have had the opposite effect. Those who advocate a woman's 'right to choose' have only been emboldened and the left-wing media is all over the pro-lifers as if they themselves pulled the trigger.

From the outer reaches of far left, evening radio talk show host Leslie Primeau has been raging at pro-lifers for not doing more to find the killer. Like as if there's something they can do that isn't already being done by the police, FBI, RCMP and everyone else involved in this thing!

Implicit in her line of thought is the idea that pro-lifers are a bunch of rednecks who hang together on Friday night and plot these things. In reality they're often people of faith who simply don't buy into the fantasy that non-living-matter can evolve into a scientist, and who take up the biblical admonition to defend those who cannot do so themselves – an amiable cause whether one is talking about babies or puppies. They are what they are because they believe in the sanctity of human life from conception to natural death, Dr. Slepian's very much included.

A true pro-lifer therefore would not have killed him, but even good causes attract fringe elements and it appears someone on that fringe did. Whether this individual's actions have an effect on the abortion rate in America is yet to be seen. What is known for sure today is that his or her actions have unquestionably cranked up the rhetoric of the pro-abort camp. One oft repeated claim made by that group is that legalized abortions save lives, and this pro-lifer frankly concedes the point.

According to Stats Canada, in the five years prior to legalization, (1964-1968) an average of nine women died each year across Canada as a result of complications from abortion. In the following quarter century that number was reduced to less than one, so it can be argued that legalization did in fact save 200 lives across the country during that period. If you think this is an unquestionably good thing, however, I know of 1.8 million fetuses aborted during the same period who would question your math... if they could.

UPDATE: As a nation, by the end of 2010 we had aborted over three million souls in this country. That's half the number of Jews killed in the holocaust – and a not insignificant number of taxpayers. Now fast forward thirty years to the day when the Canada Pension Plan has run dry for lack of contributions and conservatives are lined up with liberals for their lethal injection because society can no longer support them. On that day, we—that is, conservatives—will at least have the satisfaction of knowing who put us there. (It'll be the other guys in the queue.) And please don't misunderstand me: the damage to society from abortion is not merely some futuristic enactment of a scene from the movie *Logan's Run* (1976). No, it's now.

There is considerable evidence, for instance, of a link between a history of abortion and breast cancer. Research by Dr. Priscilla Coleman at Bowling Green State University has also found that "adolescent women who abort unintended pregnancies are five times more likely to seek subsequent help for psychological and emotional problems compared to adolescent women who carry 'unwanted pregnancies' to term."

According to a 2007 study published in *The Internet Journal of Pediatrics and Neonatology,* abortion is also associated with more frequent acts of physical aggression toward subsequent offspring. Coleman again: "The link may be influenced by a number of factors including unresolved grief... (leading to a) disruption in maternal bonding (with) subsequent born children."

Dr. David Reardon: "Previous research has also shown that abortion is linked with (an) increased risk of alcoholism, drug use, anxiety, rage, anger and psychiatric hospitalization, (any of which) individually or in combination can increase the personal and family stresses that can lead to maltreatment or neglect." It's been said that abortion involves two victims. There are, apparently, potentially many more yet.

So abortion is fatal for the fetus, deleterious for the mother and potential siblings and detrimental to the society thus robbed of his or her potential. The author sees no upside to this issue.

Euthanasia is the flipside of that coin. In Holland, where the practice has been legal since 2000, a sixteen year old can be put down without parental consent, whereas a depressed twelve year old requires it. So it would seem that dispatching the nearly dead is indeed a slippery slope to the devaluation of all life. And thus considering their effects, one might conclude that euthanasia and abortion are metaphorically the untimely-born twin offspring of the culture of death in which some are deemed less equal, less valuable, than others.

It was in a similar culture in 1780 that an admittedly self-absorbed twenty-one year old Englishman was elected to the British House of Commons where, in his words, "(His) own distinction was (his) darling object."[6] A similar culture, that is, except the babies and the aged and the understandably depressed of his day were black.

A religious conversion four years later—what he described as "the Great Change"—changed everything. But for it his life would likely be a nondescript historical footnote. Very much because of it a whole new generation is learning about the slave liberating exploits of one William Wilburforce in the movie *Amazing Grace* (2006).

It took twenty years and twelve legislative attempts, but when Wilburforce successfully brought an end to the slave trade in the British Empire in 1807, he reclined in his seat and wept. He fought on for another twenty-six years through ill health to bring an end to the institution of slavery itself throughout the Empire, thereby a few decades later earning him Abraham Lincoln's reverent approbation as the father of the abolition movement.

On subject again, if you reading this are in the midst of an unplanned pregnancy or conversely one who has already experienced the emotional trauma of abortion, I encourage you, if you so desire, to seek the counseling services offered by your nearest Pregnancy Care Center. It is a wealth of good resources and basic human compassion.

The man of many faces

June 15, 1998

Ralph Klein is a man of many faces. On one hand he can appear to be the champion of conservatism by appealing the Alberta Court of Queen's Bench ruling to read sexual orientation into the province's Individual Rights Protection Act. On the other, when it comes to actually doing something definitive and concrete like invoking the Notwithstanding Clause in the aftermath of the Vriend decision, his true colours come out.

One would be justified in believing Ralph's conservatism to be pure* because it is. As is his willingness to consult the public. Just ask the seniors. When they were consulted regarding their benefits back in '92/93 they suspected the exercise would be fruitless but went along with the process anyway, hoping against the odds to have an impact on public policy. Needless to say it was a monolithic waste of time and energy.

The findings were not what Klein wanted and twenty thousand copies of the report (save one) were shredded. So don't expect him to consult you anytime soon on the seemingly unending expansion of gay rights because a) he doesn't actually care what you think except insofar as you happen to agree with him, and b) he knows many Albertans don't. Back to Vriend.

Klein spent about a million taxpayers' dollars on the CHARADE that was his opposition to the lower court's ruling, followed by nearly $100,000 more to educate us on the virtues of the Supreme Court's identical decision.

Thus the man of many faces: one decidedly liberal; one conservative. The reality and the facade.

Speaking of conservatism—and fiscal conservatism to be precise—absolutely anyone could have balanced the budget in Alberta with the revenues we've experienced. Any elementary school-aged child could have told the bureaucrats to cut 10, 15 or 20% of their budget. A more seasoned conservative might have had the foresight to bring in an efficiency organization to study the departments and recommend where the cuts were needed. This simply makes more sense than leaving those with a vested interest in where they take place (the bureaucrats) in charge of them, which makes no sense, but that's precisely what Klein did. As it happened the bureaucrats held on to their jobs (to no one's great surprise) while those on the front lines took the big hits, adversely affecting the delivery of services.

But again we're talking about what a 'seasoned' conservative might do. Ralph Klein is the come-by-lately type who only became one following Don Getty's invitation to come feast at the cabinet table. Therein, said the man of many faces, lies my ticket to power. The rest, as they say, is history.

*This symbol did not appear in the initial column, (nothing did) but a full explanation is provided in the next.

This is (NOT) bunk

July 6, 1998

A few weeks ago in this space your amateur columnist described Ralph Klein's conservatism as 'pure'. Apparently my proofreading skills need some work because in the original text the word 'pure' preceded the word 'bunk', the latter four-letter word somehow disappearing from the published version. Oops! I shook my head in disbelief when I picked up the paper.

Readers might wonder why I pick on Ralph so much. He balanced the budget and for that we should applaud him, which I do, albeit with the understanding that anyone who couldn't do at least that in this resource-rich province should probably be institutionalized. Klein's telling the bureaucrats to trim their budgets was a no-brainer and has produced no long-term structural changes that might have ensured the ongoing affordable delivery of services. No such wisdom or forethought here, but that's not why I pick on Ralph.

One might think I do so because we don't see eye to eye on social issues like abortion and gay rights. Not so. His experience has shaped his world view, and who am I to judge him for the way he sees things? I might disagree with him wholeheartedly on many points, and I do, but I don't hold these things against him.

The reason I relentlessly hammer on Ralph Klein is because he persists in the charade that he's remotely conservative, and I don't like being lied to. An admitted Trudeau fan and lifelong card-carrying Liberal, he initially dallied with that party when making the jump from municipal to provincial politics before accepting a post as a cabinet minister in the Getty regime. This wavering between two camps would indicate to any observer that he had no solid conservative principles on which to base his future decisions. History, unfortunately, seems to have vindicated my misgivings.

UPDATE: Ralph Klein was elected mayor of Calgary in 1980 campaigning against the construction of a new city hall, only to be elected and build himself a fancy new "municipal building." Now I'm not saying that what is today colloquially referred to as the 'Taj Mahal on Macleod' (or something like it) wasn't necessary at some point, but my point is simply that this marked what was the beginning of a very long career in double-speak.

Ralph's last political act twenty-six years later was to vote against a bill that would have both allowed justices to opt out of marrying gay couples and permitted parents to excuse their children from classes in homosexual propaganda. What is noteworthy is that he did this after having built his career publicly opposing the expansion of gay rights in this country. In short, I think it's obvious on the face of it that Klein's political career was both launched and sustained by complete fabrications.

So again, why do I pick on Ralph? I do so because, as a writer, I have an obligation to bear witness to the truth, and the plain fact is: he deserved it.

The king (so named by a considerably more successful columnist than your humble scribe) is dead. Some would argue that, out of respect, I should go easy on him, but I doubt he would. Rather I suspect that he would tell me to go hard, sell lots of books and bring this message to as many as possible. I could be wrong about that, and the truth as I see it is only that, of course, but be that as it may, there's much more to follow....

Pass the buck

June 29,1998

The federal government has done what little it actually has to achieve its balanced budget scenario by cutting transfer payments to the provinces. The provinces have followed suit by passing the buck to the municipalities.

In Ontario, for example, Mike Harris has transferred 24% of provincial highways to municipal jurisdictions, which will in perpetuity be responsible for their maintenance, while at the same time keeping 100% of the fuel tax revenues in provincial coffers. Ironically, between writing the initial and final drafts of this column, your humble scribe found himself dining with Ontario's Minister of Transportation Tony Clement who confirmed these facts, adding only that a review process is in place to study the issue again in three years' time.

Our own Premier Klein took a somewhat more direct approach when he simply cut the Municipal Affairs budget by 43%. In both cases the municipal pols were sent scrambling to raise the money necessary for the delivery of services. Both governments then 'fixed' the situation by forcing their respective municipalities to adopt the system of Market Value Assessment in determining property taxes. So if I have this right, when property values rise municipal coffers will be flush and our local politicians spoiled, and when they decline the cupboards will be bare and they'll again be coming cap in hand to their provincial masters. I'm thinking there must be a better way.

Both jurisdictions are also balancing their books on the backs of the lower castes in society. The Ontario government refuses to pay for wheelchairs or wheelchair repairs, walkers, canes, hearing aids or even oxygen for anyone who isn't on welfare. I guess the working poor and retired in the heartland can do without such extravagance.

One might think 'Mike the Knife' is taking lessons from Ralph who took a round out of the primarily defenseless seniors and kindergarten students in his quest for a balanced budget. Don't get me wrong: balancing the books was long overdue, but that scenario could have been arrived at far, far more equitably.

We need governments that will balance their books on their own backs—rather than on those of the weakest members of society—and that will work diligently to pay off debts and create favourable tax climates in which the long-suffering taxpayer can simply live, work and do business. Political parties which espouse these values exist. They simply need to be embraced.

ADDENDUM: The author's objective in publishing this book has been to show how liberalism, in its various manifestations, is the scourge of western society and how "Conservatives," with rare exception, are unworthy of the name. For a better understanding of the first objective, I recommend a book entitled *The Trouble with Canada... Still!* (2010) by William D. Gairdner. It's not an easy read, (books by geniuses rarely are, this one being the obvious exception) but to suggest that it's merely worth reading would be an enormous understatement.

Taking aim at Ken

September 21, 1998

According to media reports, Alberta's former Deputy Premier Ken Kowalski is somewhat of a spendaholic with our tax dollars. During the West Edmonton Mall refinancing debacle, Finance Minister Jim Dinning fought against further exposing the public to larger losses while Ken actively promoted a "Made in Alberta" solution. In the words of the *Calgary Herald's* Don Martin, "We, the taxpayers of Alberta, stand to share the burden of Kowalski's victory."

I've been writing columns now for about four months and for a while dealing almost exclusively with the provincial Tories. They provided a great deal of fodder what with Vriend and VLTs and such, but until today I've consciously avoided dealing with King Kenny. Why make your enemies locally, I reasoned, when you can make them far away? (We live in the same small community.) His stated intention of retiring after this term was also a factor in the decision to go easy on him. The announcement that he will seek a seventh term as well as the revelation of his penchant for squandering public dough changes everything.

Anyone who's read this column for more than two weeks knows I wouldn't vote Tory if the candidate had a gun to my head. They took a province run on a pay-as-you-go basis and ran it nearly thirty billion smackerals in the hole, enslaving the unwitting borrower (you and I) to the lender.

Now it's hard not to look good while ruling the land of milk and honey, and many people still think Peter Lougheed was one of the best premiers in Alberta's history. In fact despite governing during what can be called the best of times he basically left this province on the precipice of calamity. Don Getty conversely governed during the worst of times and found himself unable to meaningfully downsize the ship of state that Peter built. That Mr. Kowalski played a significant role in these governments and therefore in the misman-agement of this province is simply an historical fact.

People say Ken has been good for the area, what with some government buildings and businesses being in the community due in some measure to his lobbying. That's only partially true if, as I maintain, he's been bad for the province. We're part of the whole and what he's done to the province he's done to us. We share in the debt he helped create and voting for him again would be akin to thanking him. Forgive me if I take a pass on this amazing opportunity to vote for my own demise.

UPDATE: Those who created Alberta's debt need to be put out to pasture, granted, but likewise those who left the province so ill prepared for the explosive growth it's experienced. And, of course, those who killed the goose that laid the golden eggs (by messing with her royalties) in order to address that growth.

In fact, former Premier Ed Stelmach was elected to lead the governing Tories in late '06 promising spe-cifically to review oil royalties, tame labour costs and address a growing housing shortage. Unfortunately he attempted to address the latter two by spiking the former, all to the significant detriment of our primary industry and the elation of other energy-producing jurisdictions which were only too happy to welcome the business. More on this in the conclusion.

Pontificating about eviscerating

July 19, 1999

The Alberta legislature's Member Services Committee, headed up by our own Ken Kowalski, voted last year to give themselves a 5% pay raise as well as a couple of other tidy little bonuses. Kowalski admitted at the time he expected to be "eviscerated" over the wage and compensation boost.

Don't run for your dictionary; I already did. Eviscerate: to remove the viscera. Well that didn't help much. Viscera: intestines. And thus the fog began to lift. I hate it when people talk over my head like that.

Ken might have read a not-so-favorable column that I, clearly his favorite constituent, penned about him some time ago, and perhaps he was thinking of me when he pontificated about being gutted like a sheep. Or not. Regardless....

Firstly, (let's ease into this) the 5% doesn't bother me much. They gave it up before asking other provincial employees to do the same and taking it back now makes them only the eighth highest paid MLAs in the country. Not a problem, but we still have the small matter of two other bonuses to deal with: one secretive; the other very lucrative.

Firstly, by tying future MLA salary increases to the Stats Canada average weekly wage index this group has virtually guaranteed themselves an annual wage increase without all the fuss of having to table it. No fuss, no muss, and importantly, no fanfare.

Due to a great deal of public pressure in '93 the Tories axed pension benefits for MLAs elected since the beginning of '89. This missed Ken who will still be collecting benefits when he retires. I don't have a huge problem with that, but it's important to know because of the second little perk this group of fiscal stalwarts have given themselves – a mere doubling of their severance package from one to now two month's pay for every year of service.

Assuming this is based on their five highest grossing years, and that the Speaker makes well in excess of $100,000 a year, and that he's been at it for around twenty, according to my rough calculations Ken's severance package just jumped from 160 to 320,000 smackerals. It could be worse. He refuses to either confirm or deny my figures. The way I see it, what he described as a done deal and not open to public debate is a shameful act of self-service.

UPDATE: After winning the 2001 election (yawn!) the Tories again increased their severance package by yet another 50% to three months pay for every year of service. The Canadian Taxpayers Federation estimated Ken's 'New Deal' (then) to be worth about five hundred grand. By the time he finally stepped down in 2012 his golden handshake from the province amounted to a cool $1.1 million, and that was on top of a $56,000/year pension he will receive, indexed to inflation naturally. Not a bad gig if you can get it.

In 2004, the CTF estimated that it would cost $17 million to retire the whole Tory crew, or about $6.00 for every man, woman and child in the province. By 2012 that amount had jumped to $25 million, or $7.35 per person. So getting rid of the Tories is kind of like buying a ticket on WestJet. The longer you wait, the more you pay – and that's just true on so many levels.

More heat for Ken

July 26, 1999

Ken Kowalski, when distancing himself from the West Edmonton Mall refinancing debacle, pointed the finger directly at Ralph Klein.

"I was not in cabinet. Who replaced me as the Minister of Economic Development on the day I was (given the boot)? It was the premier himself. He appointed himself the Minister of Economic Development." In a world where people took responsibility for what happened during their watch the buck would have stopped with Klein anyhow. As it was, even after this revelation he was still trying to squirm out from under the WEM debacle, and seemingly now has, at least for the moment. This is not about Klein.

Despite the fact Kowalski was removed from the portfolio before the proverbial manure hit the fan, his support for the deal could hardly have been clearer. "Yes, I was supportive of WEM. There's no ifs ands or buts about that". What Ken was in fact supporting was his government's practice of taxing lower and middle income Albertans for the benefit of the very wealthy who in turn finance the Tory election machine.

The self-published *Banksters and Prairie Boys* (1997) by Monier Rahall is kind of like the Bible in that it's never been proven wrong. In it Rahall highlights how the Tories have used and abused the Alberta Treasury Branch to carry out their political agenda. Are the allegations true? Following some death threats, (hardly standard procedure for the innocently accused) Moe is today living under an assumed name in the southern U.S., so it would certainly seem so.

One example noted in the book is that of a strongly worded letter by then Deputy Premier Kowalski which pressured the ATB to overturn a previously rejected $8.5 million loan application made by one Larry Ryckman. Needless to say, Ryckman got the money. This, according to Rahall, was shortly before he bankrolled Kowalski's '93 election campaign and before he went bankrupt and defaulted, the unfortunate end of much corporate welfare.

While on that subject could someone please explain to me why low and middle income families in Barrhead are taxed to expand the empire of a nearby and already substantially wealthy feed lot operator? "To create jobs," Ken would argue, and has. I beg to differ.

By propping up one the government hurts all others. By the amount they help one operator expand his herd, or increase supply, they correspondingly soften demand and reduce what all operators get for their livestock, reducing potential profits and the number of people they can employ. The net gain in employment through such government intervention is probably a calamitous loss, I don't know, but what it is for sure is an example of stealing from the poor to prop up the rich, and this cowboy is gettin' good 'n tired of it.

UPDATE: On the corporate welfare file, recall Ralph's '92 pledge to "get out of the business of being in business" – and that it was not until fourteen years later that he finally ended a hundred million dollar annual subsidy to the oil and gas industry. Public money, to friends in high places, and well greased campaigns. The only thing missing from the Adscam mix is an advertising firm.

Just call me Cassandra

January 04, 1999

Journalists rule, occasionally. You've got to go back a ways, but journalist John Robson became the ninth premier of the province of British Columbia. Prior to that province's entry into Canada his editorial arguments for Confederation earned him the opposition of those seeking to maintain the status quo, including the governor of what were then the west coast colonies, James Douglas. The man who became known as "Honest John" won the battle for the hearts and minds, got himself elected and had a mountain and park named after him. Not bad for a journalist! Most, though, are satisfied simply influencing public policy as opposed to writing it, and their pens are powerful instruments.

Two such individuals would be Bob Woodward and Carl Bernstein who together broke the Watergate story and brought down a president. Another fascinating reporter was one William Neil Connor who wrote under the byline Cassandra instead of his real name.

In pre-WWII England this Cassandra was the only writer with the spine to preach against Chamberlain's policy of appeasement toward Hitler. Most reporters of the day were in bed with the government as they depended on those officials for their headlines and thus refused to speak against them, but not him.

Cassandra fearlessly took on everybody and the paper he wrote for, *The Daily Mirror,* became the most financially successful newspaper in the history of the written word. He wrote against Chamberlain and for Churchill, essentially bringing England into the war during which he laid down his pen and took up the rifle for five years. After the war he wrote equally vociferously against Churchill and effectively had him tossed out of office. His was, apparently, a particularly powerful pen.

Klein likes to compare his battle with the deficit to Churchill's victory in Europe and has said that, unlike the British prime minister, he needs a postwar agenda to inspire the electorate. What he's doing, of course, is not so subtly comparing himself to the wartime leader.

Well, if Klein can liken himself to Churchill, you can from henceforth call me Cassandra, for it is my unwavering commitment to use this pen to promote better government, which in this case obviously necessitates bringing down a particularly poor one.

"Every man is said to have his peculiar ambition," said the twenty-three year old Abraham Lincoln in his first campaign speech... and now you know mine.

POST SCRIPT: One issue I regrettably didn't cover in these columns is education. To contribute a few words to the debate: teach, don't indoctrinate; don't pass kids who don't pass (it'll ruin them); remove those from the classroom who cannot but impede its progress; and bring back the strap – or at least untie parents' hands when it comes to administering some moderate course correction to their little charges.

In the summer of '07 an Edmonton judge lamented that he couldn't sentence the recently convicted to "a good whipping!" I don't know how busy that judge is, but I suspect if our kids were made a little more painfully aware of the difference between right and wrong, a little more often, he'd probably have more time on his hands. More on this shortly.

Like absolves like... surprised?

October 19, 1998

Recently in Saskatchewan the Crown Corporation Committee—made up largely of NDP MLAs—absolved their political masters of any wrongdoing in the botched operation and sale of Channel Lake Petroleum. I was unaware of the company before this story broke.

I'm very much aware, though, of what a cover-up smells like, and charging back bench MLAs with investigating their higher-ups inevitably leads to one. Why smear the only guy who can promote you to a comfortable cabinet post? The integrity of this group of actors aside, an absolution like this ends up looking like a whitewash whether it happens to be one or not.

Closer to home but now drifting from public memory is the Multi-Corp affair. In it both Ralph Klein's and his advisor Rod Love's wives were sold shares in the company at below market value with no money down. This was shortly before Klein himself pumped the organization in public speeches... and, predictably, before their value shot through the roof and the gals sold their shares.

The affair simply reeks to high heaven of insider trading, influence peddling and stock manipulation, but all parties were nonetheless absolved by longtime Tory Ethics Commissioner Bob Clark. Anybody's dog could see Clark was in a conflict of interest. That's his party for heaven's sake!

I believe Ralph is as guilty as the day is long, and I base this not only on the facts of the case but on the added detail that he gave the profits to charity. If I were him and were innocent I'd tell my Liberal accusers to go pound salt and would still be enjoying my good fortune. Based on my limited understanding of human nature, (picked up after thirty odd years of observing only myself, which is frankly enough to cause one to be suspect of all human behaviour) I perceive his gift not as an act of benevolence but one of contrition, tantamount to confession. This brings me to my next point.

It was necessary to bring in the Auditor General from Saskatchewan to investigate the paving of then Transportation Minister Peter Trynchy's driveway to, in Klein's own words, avoid the appearance of conflict. But in his view it's all right if our own AG investigates his role in the $400 million West Edmonton Mall fiasco? Conflict? Appearance? Fuggetaboutit!

On Multi-Corp again, if Klein were innocent he'd insist on an independent inquiry to remove any suspicion of political influence. His resistance to it is indicative of guilt. Full stop.

UPDATE: It's nice to be proven right occasionally. In his book *Left Out: Saskatchewan's NDP and the Relentless Pursuit of Mediocrity* (Indie Ink Publishing, 2010) author and radio personality John Gormley sheds light on the Channel Lake Petroleum affair noted above. According to Gormley, committee member Andrew Thomson told a gathering of constituents that the committee's final report was written before the hearings had even concluded by then Premier Romanow's Deputy Chief of Staff – who wasn't even on the committee! So the report really was a whitewash, and the self-righteous NDP have skeletons in the closet. Whodathunkit?

So many secrets

November 9, 1998

In the '70s the Liberal government of Pierre Trudeau tried to almost halve the investigative powers of Canada's Auditor General. If successful they would have simply been able to hide more of their dirty work. But for reporters keeping the issue on the front page for weeks they might have succeeded. Jean Chretien was, of course, part of that shameful debacle.

The Freedom of Information Act now limits the ability of governments to keep secrets by enabling third parties to make access to information requests and dig through the books of various departments. It's a limited success as governments have developed a habit of blacking out information in the interests of protecting personal privacy, or so they claim. What they're really hiding, of course, is anyone's guess.

A couple of years ago, for example, the feds released a 1000 plus page report on gun control with over 100 pages blacked out. What were they hiding? Knowing the Liberals I suspect it was anything that might lead you to a conclusion they didn't want you to reach.

A few years back, Alberta's then Liberal finance critic Gene Zwozdesky requested information on the Tory government's dealings in the Alpac affair. The Tories produced a ninety page document—fully half of which was blacked out—leading one to conclude that the only difference between the feds and the province in this regard is one of degree. They both have an utter contempt for the public's right to know, the Tories in Alberta only more so.

Federal NDP leader Alexa McDonough has also accused the ruling Liberals of playing hide the document in regard to the Spraypec affair. She has demanded an explanation as to why various government departments have applied to prevent the release of several memos and significantly deleted portions of eighty-four others relating to security at last year's APEC summit in Vancouver.

"We don't know the specifics of the information they've withheld," McDonough said, "but I think once again this is about protecting the prime minister from embarrassment." Undoubtedly there would be grounds for the deletion of some information regarding police sources and methods, but the temptation to hide savory details of the PM's involvement would be great.

On the home front, Klein claims the documents he's not releasing to the media regarding the WEM refinancing debacle—citing privacy concerns—he is releasing to Auditor General Peter Valentine. Obviously an independent inquiry is in order. Equally obviously it's the last thing we'll ever get from this government.

UPDATE: Got 'em! Four months into 'Honest Ed' Stelmach's regime the Alberta government released a report on oil royalties with a good chunk of it blacked out, claiming, as usual, privacy concerns. Unfortunately for the government an unedited version was filed in the departmental library where it was accessed by the opposition.

What were they hiding? Merely everything pertaining to other jurisdictions receiving higher royalties than we. This information is meaningless without a comparative analysis of the costs of extracting the stuff, but the story isn't, primarily, the royalties. It's the brazen lie that the black ink had anything to do with privacy! Busted!!

Bring back the hangman

March 01, 1999

What would happen if John King, the white suprem- acist who murdered James Bird last summer in Texas by dragging him behind his pickup truck, were a Ca- nadian and had committed this heinous deed on our soil? He'd be eligible for parole in fifteen years is what, and that, along with the grisly crime he's been found guilty of, is enough to make one quite sick. Thankfully juries in the Lonestar State have the right to execute a more fitting justice.

On the home front, the Understatement of the Year Award goes to Ralph Klein for declaring that his "Unit- ed Alternative caucus" here in Alberta is evenly split between federal Tories and Reformers – and may even contain "one or two Liberals."

Conservatives vary in how they approach the sub- ject, but most are generally agreed that reform of our flawed democratic system is required. Many endorse the principles of direct democracy—citizen's initiative, recall and referenda—any or all of which would give the voting public a measure of control over their elect- ed officials between elections and effectively end our tradition of elected dictatorships. Liberals, at least on this issue, prefer to maintain the status quo.

Three times now our liberal Tory caucus in Edmonton has defeated private members' bills calling for citizens' initiative and referenda. In those three unsuccessful attempts to improve the state of our democracy, Ralph Klein has voted against once and abstained twice while his trained seals did his bidding. The last attempt, Bill 216, was so incredibly weak I was sure they would pass it and proclaim themselves the proponents of what would in reality be only a slightly less feeble democracy. In the end even it went the way of the other two.

This column is written in response to Klein's recent posturing over the Notwithstanding Clause. A few weeks ago he assured a caller on a radio talk show that, "Yes, we could use the clause (in this case to keep same sex couples out of the domestic act) but only with permission, following full public consultation." I must have missed that call.

Of course he didn't have to consult the public after Vriend. They by the thousands contacted him of their own volition and were summarily and totally ignored. He shredded twenty thousand copies of a report on seniors' benefits when it didn't line up with his preconceived notions, and his government has defeated three bills, any one of which would have legislated our right to be heard between elections. In summary, any Tory talk of listening and caring is greatly exaggerated.

UPDATE: Not having input on important issues is one thing. Being intentionally misled on them, quite another. Albertans will recall that power deregulation was to lead to lower rates for all. The only question now that they're among the highest in the country is whether we were knowingly lied to.

As reported in the *Edmonton Sun,* then mayor Bill Smith cornered Energy Minister Steve West one day and asked him point blank if people's bills would go down. After a long pause he asked again. After another lengthy pause the minister finally responded, and I quote, "People are going to make a lot of money." I believe that answers the question.

Ferreting out Fibber Magee

March 15, 1999

For various reasons not every column I write is submitted for publication. Sometimes more important issues come up and they get bumped back. Some never see print. Such was the case with a column I wrote last year dealing with the renewed thrust in Alberta for the Tories to get with the times and support the UN Convention on the Rights of the Child, which it had until then opposed.

It, if fully implemented, would erode parents' rights to even moderately discipline their children, a position long advocated by one Dr. Benjamin Spock (1903-1998). Presumably mugged by reality, Spock recanted before his death last year, basically apologizing for screwing up an entire generation. Some disciples apparently haven't heard of his change of heart... or they simply don't care.

Visiting ultra-left-wing socialist Desmond Tutu and the opposition Liberals, for instance, blasted Klein for not getting behind said convention. Ralph stood his ground: "When do we, as parents, have rights to exercise some control and discipline over our children?" It was a straightforward statement, (posited as a question) but as I asked at the time did he mean it, or was it just a line given by a political handler to tickle the public's ears? The answer will be abundantly clear momentarily.

Time ferrets out most fibbers. It's been concealed from the media for almost two months, but in a January 13th letter to Prime Minister Jean Chretien, Premier Klein issued a strong statement of support for (you guessed it) the UN Convention on the Rights of the Child, the same document he had publicly criticized only eight weeks earlier. He expressed his government's "undivided" support for its "objectives and principles" and added that, "as a further indication of our commitment to children and families, we would like to extend our formal support for the federal government's ratification (of the deal)." In short, Ralph was feigning support for familial autonomy while almost simultaneously writing it off.

In his words, "When do we, as parents, have rights to exercise some control and discipline over our children?" We soon won't, thanks to him. As an aside, the province's opposition to the Convention was arrived at democratically during the one free vote in the legislature during the Getty years. Klein's behind closed doors reversal on this issue reveals his blatant disregard for that process.

UPDATE: In October of 2003, the United Nations issued a directive to the Canadian government that in accordance with the above noted convention, of which it was now a signatory, it must ban all forms of corporal discipline – even a slight slap on the wrist or derrière.

In the same month in which this directive was issued some high school girls in Calgary put the boots to one of their classmates because she had the audacity to tell the leader of the group, who was harassing her, to 'shut up'. This at a public train station in broad daylight! The girl was black and blue from head to torso and about a third of her hair had been ripped from her scalp.

It's probably safe to assume that five and ten years earlier these little perps were moderately more well-behaved but equally undisciplined children. It's undisciplined children, you see, who become undisciplined adolescents who beat the tar out of innocent third parties and who generally proceed to become undisciplined adults.

On the matter of discipline, we can be thankful Canada's top cops didn't just regurgitate the UN's above noted directive to ban it in its entirety, but they still went too far.

In the spring of 2004 the Supreme Court ruled that it would be crowbar hotel for anyone who applied any corporal discipline to a child below the age of two or over the age of twelve. Perhaps it's true that most children under the age of two can't cognitively connect the dots between their actions and the corresponding discipline. Perhaps it's also true that children over the age of eleven, according to a Berkeley study, are better served by reason than a sore rear end.

Perhaps, but should society criminalize a parent who taps their twenty-three month old on the pull-up to focus their attention? Or the thirteen year old who comes home from school and colourfully beaks off? There may well be better forms of punishment, but to criminalize parents for applying what for centuries has helped kids become disciplined adults is nothing short of Stalinist.

And if you believe those behind it will be content with this limited intrusion into familial life, think again. In fact the Senate Standing Committee on Human Rights regularly examines a bill that would eliminate Section 43 from the Criminal Code. Section 43, as you might guess, is precisely that which makes it legal for parents and guardians to use "reasonable force" when disciplining those in their care. No section 43; no reasonable force; no corporal discipline, period. And that's the goal!

Liberal Senator and committee member Jim Munson: "There's no such thing as 'reasonable force'" when it comes to parenting. I'm just guessing, but I suspect the elderly woman who was beaten with table legs in a Halifax park in the summer of '07, "for something to do," would probably beg to differ.

Quit yer whinin'

August 17, 1998

With all due respect the premier should stop whining for more dough from the feds and instead encourage them to get on with little things like debt and tax reduction. (Both are possible.) And then, after he stops acting like a spokesman for a special interest group, (with his hands out) he needs to look in his own backyard for constructive ways to further reduce costs and ensure the ongoing affordable delivery of services in core departments. I'm confident his spin-doctors have told him that asking for more health care dough is good politics given the concern over that issue, but there are ways to do more with less.

In that department specifically, one method to consider is the system of direct or activity based funding. In it cash follows the patient to the health care provider of choice, (rather than trickling down through the bureaucracy) ultimately causing those providers to compete for our health care dollars by providing better services and shorter waiting lists. Competition isn't a bad word, and it doesn't take a rocket scientist to see that fundamental changes need to be made to a system that forces people to wait a year and a half and more for life saving heart surgery, for but one example.

History has shown that simply throwing more money at problems doesn't solve them; it simply creates others. We need structural changes to the way things are done in this province, not bandaid solutions, and healthcare is as good a place as any to start.

Frankly I think we can expect Ralph to do some conservative things as we approach the next election, (he has some ground to make up) but adopting the system of direct funding probably won't be one of them despite Social Credit party leader Randy Thorsteinson's invitation to him to do so. To paraphrase Randy he can adopt the whole Socred platform. It's good for Albertans, so fill your boots! Apparently he's considering it.

He's considering, for instance, reducing the number of MLAs in the province. Pure Socred. It's odd that after spending a career expanding the size and scope of government, backbench MLA Peter Trynchy would introduce this legislation as a private member's bill. If the Tories were serious about it, it would be an official piece of government work, but it may yet happen.

Or maybe he'll adopt a flat tax – also Socred policy. Both moves would make him look like the conservative he's not, so I think we can almost count on them. Considering how increased provincial transfers actually hurt Alberta's bottom line, though, for optics' sake, he really should let other premiers ask for them.

UPDATE: As mentioned earlier, your author was hanging around with the Socreds when these columns were written. As you'll read in a few pages, it was also during that time the party's then leader, the aforementioned Randy Thorsteinson, quit the organization. Yours truly was pushed out the door a few years later. (You have to work pretty hard to get kicked out of a party sitting at 1% in the polls, but I managed it.) There's good and bad in everything, of course, and this means I won't be asking you, if you live in the province, to waste your vote on them. That's pos, and I'm not being spiteful. Just realistic.

Of cover ups and tax cuts

March 22, 1999

In Saskatchewan, a number of provincial Tories have been convicted of fraud. I assure you they don't have a corner on the market.

Premier Klein recently mused about striking an all-party committee to study the option of privatizing the Alberta Treasury Branch. An automated pollster has been telephoning pre-selected Albertans asking their opinion on the issue. To get the consensus he wants, (privatize) I'll lay odds that city folk with a dozen alternatives to choose from have been those most frequently quizzed. He gets the answer he seeks, does exactly as he intended in the first place and claims public support. Watch for it!

What, pray tell, is going on? The issue of privatization has never been a plank in any Tory platform and not once even breathed during an election campaign, but it seems to be a significant priority for them. Why?

Because in the books of the ATB lies the road map to where the bodies are buried. All the dirt on this government is there, but it will take what is called a forensic audit to uncover it. This gang will never order such an audit obviously, but the next one might if the bank remains in government hands, and they need to ensure that doesn't happen. It's called self-preservation.

If it ever did one could only venture a guess as to how many of our current and former Tories would be joining their Saskatchewan compatriots in the hoosegow. Maybe none. Maybe lots. A forensic audit would settle the issue. Based on their long history of non-investigations I can assure you that no such audit will occur during this government's tenure.

On the issue of budget '99 much has been said and written. Ken Kowalski: "(It's) the most outstanding budget I've experienced in terms of content and presentation in my 25 years of observation." Probably. In presentation, (hype) it's unparalleled. But all of that which is good in its content—like raising the personal exemption and flattening the tax rate—is to be implemented, if at all, in the next millennium. And that, they might as well have said, depends on oil. And the price we get for that particular commodity depends on factors outside our control such as the leaders of OPEC countries agreeing to limit production and maintaining the embargo against Iraq. They've thrown some money at health and education, but as an observant gal said to your scribe one day, whether they cut blindly as they did five years ago or throw money at problems blindly today, they're still blind.

UPDATE: Lyle Oberg would have been referring to the 'bodies' I wrote of above when in a fit of anger in early '06 he spoke about knowing where the "skeletons" are buried in this province – before furiously back-pedalling, describing the bones as merely "unfinished business." Promoted to finance minister in '07, it seems Lyle's change of heart didn't hurt his career any. Apparently in Alberta politics it's not who you know, but what you know and are willing to keep under your hat that counts. That may explain onetime minister and leadership hopeful Gary Mar's post-career succession of lucrative foreign postings, or it may not, and I'm just sayin', but it's a safe bet Mr. Oberg isn't the only former insider with the goods on this government.

Of napalm and health care

July 05, 1999

In the '60s, President Lyndon Johnson and Secretary of Defense Robert Macnamara micro-managed Vietnam from Washington. They called the shots while the hamstrung generals in the field merely relayed their messages. That neither had a shred of actual military experience might explain why the war was an unqualified disaster. Believe it or not there's a parallel between this and Alberta Health.

The Klein revolution in the mid '90s produced seventeen arbitrarily defined regional health boards in the province manned entirely by Tory hack appointees. Continuing with the analogy, they're the generals, and contrary to promises made at the time there's not a duly elected soul among them. All therefore owe their allegiance to he who, through them, micro-manages the system from Edmonton. Kinda like 'nam.

It's a bit of a digression, but this puts to naught Ralph's cry for greater democracy during the run-up to Alberta's senatorial race last year. It was federal, it wouldn't take away from his powers, and it made him look good, so he promoted it. Meanwhile back at the ranch, we the unwashed masses wait in vain for the opportunity to actually vote for someone to sit on these boards.

At the time of this writing two of these fifteen member boards have been replaced by what we presume is a capable individual, begging the question of why we had so many on them to begin with. If one person can undo the mess of fifteen, couldn't such an individual run the system better in the first place?

So it would seem that we don't need fifteen well-heeled appointed Tory hacks on each of seventeen boards sucking the public teat. Nor do we need the boards themselves. One board consisting of five retired doctors would suffice while saving the bedraggled tax-payer a small bundle.

What's the real purpose of these boards? I suspect it's simply to deflect heat. You see the nurses' unions don't fight the government for more dough; they fight the boards while our elected reps, who are supposed to be defending the public purse, watch from afar. Because the board members are appointed, and thus as I wrote earlier beholden to him who done it, Klein can call the shots while appearing to be detached from the situation. Diabolically ingenious, I say.

Ralph's revolution, including the creation of these boards, was an experiment in health care re-engineering. In your humble scribe's opinion the experiment has been a disaster and the boards—all of them—should be shown the door.

UPDATE: In 2001, Premier Klein finally fulfilled an early campaign promise when two thirds of the board members in the province were elected. Nineteen months later the whole lot were fired! Elected or not, it appears dictators don't like what they can't control.

Now this might seem like a bit of a segue, but your humble scribe spent the first decade and a half of this millennium selling earlier editions of this book door to door. One advantage of this somewhat unique livelihood has been the people he's met along the way whose stories sometimes appear in these pages.

Though his form of rebellion is no longer pertinent, (as they've been eliminated in the province) one such person was a man who refused to pay his Alberta Health Care premiums. (The author does not advocate tax evasion, but readers in B.C. and Ontario might want to listen up.) Instead he paid as he went when requiring medical attention and disregarded the government's hate mail.

To make a long story short he had a hernia and because he wasn't insured didn't have to line up like the rest of us. It was fixed in two weeks instead of six months, at a cost of $800—charged to him—instead of $3000 the doctor would have charged the system. The extra billing, explained the doctor, is because the government makes him wait six to nine months for payment. His costs, alternatively, are up front (nurses wages, operating facilities, etc).

So why does health care cost so much in this country? There are myriad reasons obviously, but bureaucratic delay is clearly one of them. Do you think maybe leaving those bureaucrats in charge of the cutbacks in the mid-nineties was just a little shortsighted?

If that was a faux pas, firing a few dozen in '08, replacing what were by then nine regional entities with one superboard may yet prove to be a step in the right direction – if it doesn't lead to more micro-management. But apparently that's exactly what it's done.

One day someone from the new office called a ward nurse to confirm that the ordered stethoscopes were for medical purposes. "Of course not," replied the quick witted nurse, "they're for Halloween costumes!" To the best of the author's knowledge we are the only species in creation with the gift of humour. When 51% of our exploding health care budget is consumed by administration, it comes in handy sometimes.

Bureaucrats – the unscathed menace

July 12, 1999

In 1998, the Provincial Health Council of Alberta stated that the wrenching health care reforms of the past few years were a good start but not enough to stave off a potential collapse of the system. "It is our judgment that the health system as it is currently organized today is not sustainable in the long run," concluded acting chairman Gail Surkan. And of course she's absolutely right!

Unfortunately the politicians have again lined up to throw money at the situation, thus once again merely kicking the ball down the field. (It's what they do best.) The result of the much ballyhooed Social Union summit last year, for instance, was more federal (make that, taxpayer) cash for the health system. And the main point of Klein's last state of the union address was more provincial (same taxpayer) cash for front line services. That, of course, is where all the money he yanked from the system came from, but is the money actually necessary?

Unequivocally 'yes' if we're going to stick with the collapsing system described by Ms. Surkan in the opening paragraph. That system requires scads of money to forestall the aforementioned collapse, but that's all it does. Why? Because in Klein's little revolution he failed to address the real problem besetting the department: the proliferation of bureaucrats.

They, left in charge of the cuts, ensured their jobs were safe (who wouldn't?) while those on the front line and otherwise lower down the totem pole took the hits. I've mentioned it before, but would it not have been far more effective to have hired an efficiency organization to study the department and recommend where the cuts were needed? Some nurses might have lost their jobs, granted, but a great many bureaucrats would most certainly have lost theirs. Another alternative would have been to embrace what's known as direct or activity-based funding. In it, funds follow the patient to the provider of choice, thus circumventing the bureaucracy making not a few of their jobs redundant.

Either of the above suggestions would have begun to deal with the bloated system we're forced to support. Instead our premier opted to leave the foxes in charge of the chicken coop, no systemic changes were made and the department will require more and more and more loot to stave off its inevitable collapse. It's simply too top heavy, and that has yet to be dealt with.

UPDATE: The Fraser Institute released a study in August 2000 which tracked health funding across the country between 1993 and 1998. It found that contrary to popular wisdom, provinces with higher per capita health spending had longer, not shorter, waiting lists and concluded that the current system is "grossly dysfunctional." Regardless, every gabfest on the subject results in yet more money being thrown into this black hole while our waiting lists continue to grow.

In a study entitled *How Good is Canadian Health Care,* (2004) the Fraser Institute again showed clearly how little we get for our health care dollars. Despite being tied with Iceland for having the most expensive health care system in the industrialized world, we endured "mediocre health outcomes, some of the longest wait times in the world and terrible access to doctors and technology." In 2010, again according to the number-one-ranked think tank in Canada according to a University of Pennsylvania study, we paid for the sixth-most expensive health insurance system among 28 OECD countries and yet ranked close to the bottom of the pack in the aforementioned outcomes.

Why? Because of a lack of competition in the delivery of health services as enjoyed by every other country in the OECD... and, I add, bureaucrats. Every government needs good ones. We simply have too many, consuming far too many scarce health care dollars.

ADDENDUM: The bureaucracy is one problem; unions are another. During the Mulroney years, a civil servant's job was eliminated, but he remained. And played chess. Eight hours a day. Seriously!

In 2011, another was found spending five hours a day responding to and sending illicit pornographic pics and messages. Like the chess player, he too still has his job, such being the power of unions.

Note that unions all but killed GM by demanding exorbitant salaries and benefits for blue-collar labour, and they make the firing of rogue employees well-nigh impossible. Well, 'nigh' impossible anyway.

One day a union boss showed up at a construction site with a "Proud to be Union" sticker for everyone's hard hat. From high atop a wall he was building, one rather outspoken amateur steel worker yelled something to the effect that it would be a cold day in hell before he would advertise such rubbish, and that was the end of him. Fortunately the author didn't much like that job anyway and will return to the subject of unions in the conclusion.

Divided we fall – or not

May 26, 1999

Two weeks ago, Social Credit Party leader Randy Thorsteinson gave the conservative movement in Alberta a black eye when he quit and ran off with a number of people to start another party.

The schism stems from what at first appears to be some people's religious intolerance. The executive of the Rocky Mountain House Constituency Association raised the issue of the concentration of Mormons on the party's executive. Being one, Randy took it kind of personally and quit. Before even becoming aware of that point, though, he had already stormed out of the meeting when long time candidate Laverne Ahlstrom refused to sign his own nomination papers fully two years before an election was anticipated.

Already in his mid-sixties, Ahlstrom reasoned that if a younger, more qualified man or woman came along he'd prefer to hand over the reigns: a thoroughly understandable position to everyone except Randy. He overreacted not only to that, but also to point five on the agenda for the evening questioning the wisdom of having a disproportionate representation of Mormons on the board.

The two sides in this conflict are not equally at fault. The RMH folk were not questioning Randy's faith but rather the political perception of having a concentration of people from any particular group on the executive, be they Atheists, Baptists or Tiddly Winks players. Regardless of 'who started it', what they've managed to do is give themselves is a big fat PR headache.

Can any good come from this? Of course! I'm not sure exactly how just yet, but neither was a young man named Joseph when he was languishing in an Egyptian prison on trumped up charges some 4,000 years ago. I had to go back a ways to find an example of a bad thing becoming a good thing, but as it turned out his circumstances led to the very survival of the people of Israel and Egypt. Archeological evidence, as usual, verified the biblical account, in this case the discovery of coins inscribed with his name and what is presumably his likeness. Old Joe, of course, could have had no idea where his incarceration would lead.

And nor can we know how this schism in Alberta's right will unfold. Time alone will tell. Randy's a good party leader but not indispensable. (No one is.) I suspect in the long run he's done more damage to his own political aspirations than to the conservative movement in the province, but time will tell.

UPDATE: The right as I mentioned earlier was getting a little crowded in Alberta in '07. As reported it thinned somewhat in '08 with the merger of the Alberta Alliance and Wildrose parties under the banner of the Wildrose Alliance Party of Alberta. (Full disclosure: your humble scribe was a founding member of both the Wildrose and the combined entity.)

Since its inception in 2002, the Alliance, begun by the aforementioned Thorsteinson, had been strong on policy but constitutionally weak as that document rested all authority in its leadership. Newly formed in 2007, the Wildrose Party was alternatively governed by a very sound constitution that rested the same in its membership where it belonged. Combining the policies of the former with the bylaws of the latter was a good move – and frankly this has potential... but not necessarily for good.

The Tories in this province are as liberal as the day is long, (I hope that point has been adequately made) but is the Wildrose any more conservative?

In fact, leader Danielle Smith has long endorsed gay marriage, a woman's right to choose and legalized brothels. After the 2012 election she was also willing to jettison that party's rightly skeptical stand on global warming, force marriage commissioners and nurses to violate their consciences if they wanted to keep their jobs and to finance sex change operations. In short she's about as conservative as Olivia Chow, the failed Toronto mayoral candidate and widow of former NDP leader Jack Layton, both of whom you'll read about in a couple of pages. And as the author feared when she ran for the leadership of the Wildrose in 2010, Danielle has basically managed to mold the once conservative party into her image.

Discouraged by the vacuum on the right in the province, Thorsteinson is back in the game and organizing the Reform Party of Alberta. As they say, it ain't over 'til the fat lady sings, and I'd like to think she hasn't even started warming up yet.

Later in life, Winston Churchill, who was himself no stranger to electoral defeat, was asked to give the commencement speech at his old alma mater. It's likely the shortest commencement address ever recorded: "Never, never, never, never give up!" And with that he sat down. So don't give up, ever, but note to Wildrose: when you find yourself looking exactly like everyone else in the room, it's probably a good time to take a long look in the mirror and question your raison d'être?

Socialists and other monkeys

August 02, 1999

Radio commentator Paul 'and now you know... the rest of the story' Harvey tells of an experiment involving a chimpanzee scientists were determined to teach written communication. For fourteen years project directors worked patiently with the chimp providing it with things in its cage to enable it to form words.

When word went out that this primate had finally constructed a sentence from the symbols it had been learning, many scientists gathered around the cage. You can only vaguely imagine the excitement in the room when the little guy approached his work, took a short bow and threw off the veil. And the primate's first words? "Get me the h-e-double-hockey-sticks outta here!"

Fabricated, sure, but a great story. The fictitious monkey might have been the best treated primate in history, but it was meaningless to him without freedom. All he cared about was getting out of his cage. Such is the inherent, unanswerable problem of socialism.

Socialist goals seem reasonable enough – basically to provide a decent standard of living for all. Unfortunately while trying to provide such, socialist governments thoroughly undermine their citizens' economic freedom. You see, governments don't have anything they didn't first take from someone else, and by providing goodies for all they first have to take them away from those who honestly earned them, thus destroying an essential element of any successful society: incentive.

Why put in long hours or develop new technologies if the fruits of your labour will be confiscated by the state? As I said, socialists have amiable goals like ending poverty and such, but in their efforts to promote an egalitarian society, (where all enjoy an equal outcome) sweat equity and hard work become a distant memory.

Workers in the Soviet Union said it well: "They pretend to pay us – we pretend to work." The result was an industrial sector that had barely moved beyond the industrial revolution when the Iron Curtain finally fell. Remember, even though he lived in the most opulent monkey digs, all the little fella' ever really wanted was his freedom. Think about it.

ADDENDUM: Socialism can be loosely defined as a system of governance in which the state controls the means of production in society, be that through outright ownership of the same or through an equally unworkable, centrally planned economy. Communism is all that and more at the end of a bayonet. For the finer differences between these philosophies, I encourage you to consult someone who has belonged to the parties that espouse them. His name is Brian Mason, he led the socialist NDP in Alberta from 2004-2014, is a former member of the Communist Party of Canada and the fruit that didn't fall far from the tree.

Or Ann McGrath, Chief of Staff to then national leader Jack Layton and a former member of the Communist Youth League. Or Olivia Chow whose campaigns are regularly staffed by communist volunteers. As-were-her-late-husband's! How do I know? A good friend of mine used to be one of those volunteers! He saw the light and became a conservative, a fact undoubtedly contributing to our friendship. Needless to say, my relationship with the others mentioned here, save Jack, is just a little strained at the moment.

Every job has an upside

September 07, 1998

As an older and wiser friend once said, "Every job has its pros and cons. One needs to make the most of the former and minimize the latter." One of the pros of my particular line of work with the Canadian Taxpayers Federation is the people it brings me into contact with. One such person was John Moerman, a former member (now deceased) and the very fine individual whose columns used to appear in this space.

Another would be Carol Farnalls, the publisher of *The Barrhead Leader* who graciously publishes these humble efforts. I mean seriously: how often does a high school educated guy with an axe to grind get the opportunity to publish his thoughts every week?

It has also been my great pleasure to come to know the affable and charming local columnist over there to my right—your left—Carolyne Aarsen. She's a sweetie.

At a recent Taxpayers conference I was privileged to meet Ontario's Minister of Transportation, Tony Clement, a bright fellow who in my opinion is a likely successor to Mike Harris as leader of that province's Conservative party. On the last evening of the conference it was also a great pleasure to dine with and get to know one Stephen Harper. Stephen, a former Reform MP and policy advisor, is the current president of the National Citizens Coalition.

The Taxpayers' board of directors work without remuneration. They contribute their experience and expertise to the organization simply for the satisfaction of contributing to its success. It's been good to get to know them. Among that group is former Conservative cabinet minister and Iron Lady of Alberta politics, Connie Ostermann. And I do mean 'Iron Lady'.

As a minister this thorn in Don Getty's side opposed just about everything he did, but hers was a lone voice in cabinet. Her reward for bucking the trend was to be given the relevant portfolio six months before the Principle Group (Lougheed's made in Alberta financial empire) hit the wall, an event Getty had to know well in advance was coming.

In Connie's words she resigned in May of '92 because in good conscience "(she) couldn't support the ongoing business investments, huge deficits and lack of accountability which characterized the Conservative government." It's said her departure led directly to Getty's resignation as they couldn't find anyone in her riding to represent the party while he remained at the helm. "If there's any truth to that," says Connie, "(she) should have left a lot sooner."

As the heading of this column points out, every job has an upside. The best part of mine is the literally hundreds of people it gives me a chance to meet. The foregoing has just been a smattering of them, but space is limited.

ADDENDUM: It's always encouraging to learn that someone has saved your column, for whatever reason. In the Aarson household, for instance, whenever the aforementioned Carolyne's sweetness is questioned, she just pulls out this one and explains to the doubting Thomases that clearly she is – and there it is in black and white for all to see. That story was just too cute to not include here. And now, to federal and international issues.

Fix Canada

Federal and International Issues

Child care conspiracy

June 8, 1998

One can be forgiven for thinking there's a conspiracy going on around here. In a study entitled The Benefits and Costs of Good Child Care, authors Michael Krachinsky and Gordon Cleveland conclude that there is a $2 savings in labour productivity and decreased social costs for every $1 the government invests in 'quality' child care. The solution? More money for it, naturally.

Another report by the feds concludes that child care workers are woefully underfunded, and National Crime Prevention Council research shows that negative childhood experiences are closely linked to latter criminal behaviour. These studies may be entirely sound, but their authors seek more than mere mammon. They want nothing short of a national tax-funded universal daycare program and we're being inundated with messages for its need.

Some argue the traditional, single income family is under attack by those who advocate such a program. The problem, they claim, is that the taxes of the already beleaguered single income family will be further increased to expand the subsidy to their dual income neighbours benefiting from the program, an inequitable transfer of funds from those who make sacrifices to keep one parent at home to those who do not. And they're absolutely right.

Reform MP Eric Lowther correctly contends that the government needs to extend a child care credit to "ALL parents, including those who care for their children at home, instead of further straining the most critical relationship in the long term health of society: the parent-child bond." Plato, who advocated removing all children from the family unit and having them reared entirely by the state, would be pleased with the proposed developments in Canada. Those who recognize the need for such bonding should be anything but.

On a positive note, Dr. Kyle Pruett's study at Yale's Child Study Center concludes that children raised by men (yes Virginia, men) "are often active, vital and vigorous" and show a particular interest in "the external environment." Can you say, 'politics'? Perhaps the fact that my father was very instrumental in raising me is the reason you're reading this column today.

Studies also show how the nurturing activities of both parents stimulate the emotional attachment so vital in the development of personality in the early years. The changing faces of daycare workers can't replace that, so if staying at home with them is an option... take the option. The benefits could be inestimable.

ADDENDUM: The Swedish government provides virtually free day care for all preschoolers sixteen months of age and older. To finance this and other lavish programs, their parents' tax rates are among the highest in the world, forcing both to work, which in part explains why 92% of qualifying preschoolers in that country find themselves in said care. And the outcome? Education standards are falling while psychosomatic disorders among Swedish youth are climbing at a faster rate than in comparable European states. If these facts are related, then it would seem that making child rearing a state responsibility is precisely the costly, destructive, liberal misadventure conservatives have always said it is. Note: this doesn't make conservatives smart... just caring.

Indifference to our political system

July 13, 1998

No mortal is going to create a political utopia, but that doesn't excuse anyone from doing what he or she can to contribute to the improvement of society. For most that means we work, pay taxes, support some good causes and go to the polls on election day and make an informed decision. I would that it were so.

Many obviously fail to stay abreast of political issues and sleepwalk to the polls if they go at all. You can see evidence of this (dare I call it) ignorance when a week before a federal election the CBC can gather together a room full of people who still don't know how they're going to vote to listen to the rhetoric of the various parties. That general ignorance of political issues is why we have a Liberal government in Ottawa today, and it's 2.2 million Ontarians who made it possible.

I guess they just forgot about Chretien's three promises that won him the '93 election. If you recall, they were to eliminate the GST, create jobs, jobs, jobs and restore integrity to the PMO, not one of which were fulfilled. He denied ever making the first promise, real unemployment remains naggingly high and, forgive him, he probably never understood the meaning of the word 'integrity', what with his difficulty with the language and so on. Allow me to explain what integrity is not, Mr. Chretien....

Integrity is not... making up a story about slipping away from Sussex Drive to visit a homeless man. (His aides have admitted that this story, told to a group of students in Manitoba, was a complete fabrication.) It's also not paying off your adversary to run a lame duck campaign as is told you did in Shawinigan during your first two campaigns. A man has admitted that in collusion with Chretien and in exchange for a job in the national parks for his son, he secured the Conservative nomination in the riding in 1963 and again in '65, and in both cases proceeded to give no interviews, partake in no debates and knock on no doors, basically ensuring our current PM's success.

Frankly I wouldn't buy a used car from the man, let alone trust him or any other Liberal to run my country. Nor a 'Progressive', regardless of his limited experience in the job. (Hi Joe!). We're in the predicament we're in today because of 130 odd years of Liberal and Tory misrule. To continue to bounce between those parties and expect good government one day would be the height of naiveté. To produce different results, obviously we need to start doing things differently.

At the top of this column I wrote that we all need to do what we can to contribute to the improvement of society. I believe Preston Manning did just that when he created the Reform Party of Canada. His creation is far from perfect obviously—it was made with human hands after all—but for my money it's light years ahead of the competition in promoting good policy.

UPDATE: After all of the above, does a little thing like overpaying ad agencies to circuitously finance election campaigns with public money—the crux of Adscam—really surprise anyone? It shouldn't. It's the Liberal way.

Unite the right

July 20, 1998

Joe Clark's stated intention in seeking the leadership of the Progressive Conservative Party of Canada (again) is to keep the right disunited and thus, I presume, keep the Liberals in power indefinitely.

That he will win against the current crop of candidates is beyond doubt. Rightly or wrongly, Joe will win. It's foreordained – which is why Reformers need to take decisive action.

To continue to do business as usual would be to invite Joe to erode the party's soft support to the consternation of the country's true conservatives – and the elation of the Liberals who would look on their reign as bordering on eternal. The decisive action required on the part of Reform... is dissolution.

To stop the aforementioned scenario from unfolding, Preston or Deborah or Stockwell could run for the leadership of the Tory party, and Reformers across the country could take out PC memberships to ensure that their man or woman won the crown. They'd whip the capital 'C' conservatives who would be greatly outnumbered and... Voila!! We have one right wing party to chase the Liberals into exile in the next election.

It's not a bad plan methinks, but maybe it's not necessary. Maybe the Tories under Joe Who won't erode their support, and maybe the Liberals will mess their diapers so bad before the next election that people will flock to Reform, but that's a lot of maybes. I think Reformers best do everything in their power to unite the right and do it now. If that means swallowing their pride and changing their name, so be it. Desperate times require desperate measures, and I reckon these times qualify.

Manning might also consider stepping aside. He took the party from nowhere to being the official opposition in ten years and for that true conservatives should always be grateful, but even he must realize he has some personal characteristics that the style-conscious Canadian public reject.

They want style, not substance, and for a person with the latter—substance—to be elected, it seems he has to be able to deliver it with a good deal of the former – style. (Chretien is an anomaly, having neither.) Maybe Stock Day will take a run at it. Or maybe it's time Canada had its own version of an Iron Lady. Or maybe I'm dreaming that Reform will even consider these ideas. I hope they do. I'd like to see good government in my day. Doc Thiessen says I've only got forty years.

UPDATE: Mission accomplished... sort of. It wasn't quite what I had in mind, but the Tory and Alliance (nee, Reform) parties did successfully merge in December '04 under the banner of the Conservative Party of Canada. They formed a minority government in January '06 and were rewarded with an increased minority in October '08. Faced with the prospect of losing their allowance, (a $2.00 per vote political party welfare subsidy created by Jean Chretien) the leaders of the three opposition parties then tried to effect an unarmed coup. The coup failed, but the greedy whiners got to keep their loot, thus giving the Tories a marketable wedge issue in the 2011 election that finally saw them attain majority status. That hard work done, 'progressives' like Peter McKay reportedly lie awake at night dreaming of a reverse takeover of the party. The price of freedom, as they say, is indeed eternal vigilance.

ABC: Anybody But Clark

February 08, 1999

I stayed up to watch the 11:00 PM news one Sunday night in November and was treated to an interview with newly-elected Progressive Conservative Party leader Joe Clark. To make sure I had the quotes right I parted with $15.00 and ordered the transcript. (Coincidentally the exact amount I'm paid to write this column, so this one's on the house.)

To be clear, let me state at the outset that Clark lost the PM's job in 1980 because he can't count. He called a critical vote on a budget when he didn't have enough bodies in the house to ensure its passage, thus enabling the Liberals to shoot it down and waltz back into the halls of power. (And thus we can thank Joe Clark, indirectly, for the NEP, but I digress.) And now to the interview:

In it Clark states, "My reputation became stronger during the period when I was foreign affairs minister and constitutional minister... I have to try to continue to approach Canadians in the spirit that I did in (those) incarnations." Spare us!

In his so-called 'incarnation' as foreign affairs minister, Clark, in 1986, gave $60 million to the Mengistu Haile Mariam regime of Ethiopia, the same year that government spent $100 million on arms to suppress its own people. One can only guess at how many perished in that politically motivated famine as a result of our minister's misguided benevolence.

As Captain Canada, our constitutional affairs minister presided over the doomed Charlottetown Accord.

A poll taken at the time showed Joe to be even more popular than Brian Mulroney. It's just a minor detail, of course, but so was I.

In the aforementioned accord the government tried to create a dozen more federal ridings in our already significantly over-governed country and a whole new level of government to look after native affairs. Thankfully the majority of clear-thinking Canadians in all parts of the country shot that baby out of the sky, natives included. In none of these incarnations has Clark engendered anything closely approximating a sense of confidence. Derision, yes; confidence, not so much.

Back to the interview: "I very much hope that I can appeal to people in their hundreds of thousands who voted Reform, as indeed I want to appeal to people who voted for the Bloc Québecois, who voted for the Liberal party, for the NDP or people who simply didn't vote in the last election." The trouble with trying to appeal to everyone, of course, is that one ends up standing for nothing, which unfortunately pretty much sums up Joe Clark. God help this country should he ever regain a position of influence within it.

You can tell a lot about people by whom they support politically. Both Peter "the Pink" Lougheed and Ralph Klein have publicly declared their support for Joe. In light of the above observations, this belies their claim to be conservative thinkers. Liberal stinkers rhymes, and seems far more apropos.

UPDATE: In the summer of 2010, former Liberal leader Jean Chretien, former NDP leader Ed Broadbent—and the aforementioned Joe Clark—got together to discuss creating a united, left-wing party to take on the Tories. Enough said... about Joe Clark. I will return to the subject of the proposed merger shortly.

Chretien stokes separatist fires

September 28, 1998

What's the difference between Trudeau's middle-finger salute to western Canadians and Chretien's bludgeoning Alberta's Senate election process two weeks ago? Not much!

By appointing nuclear disarmament activist Doug Roche to the sleepy second chamber when an election to fill the vacant seat was imminent, our prime minister basically flipped us the bird and once again stoked the fires of western separation. The main question on the street the day following the appointment was not 'if' but 'when' we would have a say in our role in Confederation.

Western Canadians in particular (maybe that 'w' will be permanently capitalized one day) are fed up with the dictatorial powers our democracy bestows on its leaders and we'll have change or eventually we'll have none of it. We will not continue down the path of elected dictatorships indefinitely while a party which advocates positive democratic change continues to be rejected because of its place of birth.

And what a difference a few years can make! In 1991, while in opposition, Chretien stated that a "reformed" Senate is essential, adding that it must be "elected, effective and equitable." Today he can be heard saying the election process is "ridiculous" and that "you can't elect senators in one place and not another." Really?

The PM would be well aware that the first American senators weren't elected. In 1904, Oregon (that rebel) held the nation's first senatorial elections. Many western states followed suit and in 1913 the 17th Amendment to the Constitution required all states to elect their senators.

So YES YOU CAN elect senators in one place and not another, and there is tremendous precedent for what we've been doing in Alberta right on our southern border. Chretien is apparently willing to deny any knowledge of this easily known fact in an attempt to maintain his dictatorial powers of appointment. And he's not the only one spinning a yarn here....

I would hope that conservatives see that Ralph Klein's championing the cause of Senate reform is merely a ploy to restore his weakening credibility as a reformer. Any doubts about his motives were dispelled when Alberta's Intergovernmental Affairs Minister Dave Hancock phoned Mr. Roche to congratulate him on his appointment and express his government's support for the same. "In fact," says Roche, "the word they used was 'delighted.'"

"Delighted." It's funny how one word can wreck the most well laid plans. My appreciation to Dave Hancock for spilling the beans on the Tory government's true feelings on this issue.

UPDATE: Speaking of Dave Hancock, do you remember the Jabergate affair? I'm bouncing back to a provincial issue here, but it's worth a look.

In 2001, Ziad Jaber was convicted of influence peddling and fined $161,000 for accepting a $200,000 bribe to secure a lease for a prospective tenant who simply wanted to open a liquor store in a Fort Saskatchewan strip mall. Premier Klein's response to this issue when it first surfaced was that he had nothing to hide, and I quote, "on this one." I couldn't make this stuff up!

The lamestream media again went mute on the issue, but if Klein had nothing to hide, "on this one," it could only be because he did on other issues. Three words can imply volumes. Just ask Mr. Hancock.

When questioned as to why it took a $200,000 greasing of the palms to secure a lease in a mall for a liquor store, then Justice Minister Hancock responded that it was a "very silly question." It would only be one, of course, if this was business as usual in what was Ralph's World. Otherwise it was actually a pretty good one.

True to form, Klein refused to call a public inquiry into the matter. If he had, someone would have undoubtedly asked an embarrassing question as to why he hadn't for issues he very much did have his fingers in, Multi-Corp and WEM coming readily to mind.

Ralph's three words, "on this one," point to his own culpability on other issues. Dave's indicate systemic corruption. I'm 'delighted' they chose to use them.

FURTHER UPDATE: On the matter of Senate reform, (which is where this column began) much has been made of Stephen Harper's appointment of a number of senators despite promises of reform. The fact is he had been pushing for such reform for years, unsuccessfully, precisely because of the number of Liberals in the Upper House. To risk those seats being filled by yet more Liberals at some future date would be stupid – and they don't call Harper the "evil genius" for nothing. On the question of abolition, (pushed to the fore by some of Harper's more questionable appointments) can you imagine a country governed by Trudeau the Lesser *without a chamber of sober second thought?* Perish the thought I say, and long live a reformed Senate. It might come in handy one day.

Grits, Tories and dinosaurs

October 12, 1998

Six Armed Forces personnel died recently when their thirty-plus year old helicopter exploded over the Gaspé Peninsula. The saddest part of all this is that the crash, if as presumed the result of mechanical failure, was entirely preventable.

If the Mulroney Conservatives hadn't balked for years about replacing those aging choppers, these guys would have been flying a state-of-the-art machine instead of the jalopy that became their casket. The timing of that decision gave the Liberals an opportunity to make an extremely irresponsible campaign promise to scrap the deal to buy the replacement EH-101, a promise they fulfilled to the detriment and endangerment of every Air Force helicopter pilot and serviceman in Canada.

The Tories' dithering on this file was one thing, (they had budget issues to contend with following the profligate Trudeau years) but the Liberal's cancellation of the deal was an example of almost breathtaking stupidity. Before going on to another issue let me state that the dead may have done more for their country in dying than many of us do in the living if, as more people become aware of its role in this disaster, their deaths lead to the fall of this government.

On another matter, as of this writing Liberal Finance Minister Paul Martin wants to transfer a $20 billion surplus in the EI fund into general revenues where it can be squandered on vote buying schemes. I can't speak for anyone else obviously, but I pay EI premiums as a form of insurance against unemployment, not to help Liberal governments buy the votes of them who are so easily duped by their schemes.

For this, for cancelling the helicopter purchase further endangering the lives of our servicemen and for a thousand other plainly destructive things they've done over the years, the Liberals should be sent the way of the Tories and the dinosaurs. It will be a fine day if and when that happens. It's just a great shame that it might take the deaths of six innocent servicemen to wake this country from its political lethargy.

UPDATE: Smart people learn from other people's mistakes; Liberals appear to have a hard time learning even from their own. In fact, even after the $500 million fiasco that was the EH-101 cancellation, they were again threatening to cancel the super cool F-35 contract at an estimated cost of $300 million according to figures published in the *National Post,* if and when re-elected.

So why do those who do, continue to vote Liberal? Ignorance. (Obviously the author, who is ignorant of a great many things—not the least of which is aircraft specs—uses the term in its non-accusatory form.) In fact a U.S. study has shown that the more people read, the more knowledgeable they become on a specific issue, the more conservative they tend to become on that issue. They might still be considered liberal generally, but on that issue at least they become less so. To suggest that people vote liberal due to ignorance is therefore not an insult but rather a genuine observation. There is a painless antidote to this condition—it's called reading—but what one reads is every bit as important as the act itself, and with all due respect to authors Michael Ignatieff and Naomi Klein, vacuous, anti-American Marxist pap should probably be left on the shelf.

Hats off to George

February 01, 1999

George Harris, a Winnipeg office worker, is suing the feds for their failure to collect capital gains on $2.2 billion moved out of the country in 1991. The family who did this deed can't officially be identified under Revenue Canada's confidentiality rules, but unofficially the family name is Bronfman, or so it's widely assumed.

In 1991, the federal Tories let them walk without paying $700 million in taxes arguably owed on the fund, and today the Liberals are fighting for the family's right to keep the loot. Tell me again, Mr. Chretien, what exactly is the difference between your party and the one you supplanted in '93? Both seem to be manned by bandits who rob from the poor and let the rich get away scot-free. Go get 'em, George!

This situation reveals two things that historically have been wrong with Confederation. One is that there is absolutely no difference between the two mainline parties, leaving Canadians for generations past little choice but to vote for bad government. (Yes, we had the New Democrat alternative, but not for anyone willing to think through their more overtly socialist policies.)

The other historical problem referred to is that we have government of, by and for the wealthy at the expense of the poor and middle class. Letting the Bronfmans who have long supported both major parties off the hook is but one example. Providing an interest free loan to Bombardier two years ago is another. It was interest free to them only. You and I foot that bill.

Prime Minister Chretien has announced that he will spend $500,000 to find out why western Canadians feel alienated and discontent. The why, Mr. Chretien, is because you waste our hard-earned tax dollars on ridiculous studies like this! Call off this futile waste of money and phone me. I'll give you a dozen reasons for national discontent, not merely western, and it won't cost you a dime.

There are myriad problems with Confederation. We in the west are generally willing to try to fix them, which is why we vote as we do, but our patience has its limits. If central and eastern Canadians continue to foist Liberal governments on us, that alone should frankly qualify as grounds for divorce one day. Why? Because no self-respecting people should tolerate, indefinitely, the abuse of their and their children's pocketbooks inherent in liberal governance. So it's change or bust eventually, take your pick. It also so happens that dissolution is entirely feasible from a western standpoint. The continued election of Liberal governments in Ottawa, I believe, simply draws the day ever nearer.

UPDATE: Note that the election of the federal Conservatives in January '06 at least temporarily halted separatist sentiment in both the west and Quebec. Note also the explosion of that sentiment in both when a liberal coalition tried to usurp power in 2008. Why the strong reaction? Je ne parle pas pour Québec, but I suspect many westerners would frankly rather pack their bags than repeat the dark night of the soul that was both the Trudeau and the Chretien/Martin era. Early in his tenure, Liberal leader Michael Ignatieff claimed that maintaining national unity was his party's highest priority. That can't be true, of course, for nothing could drive western separatist sentiment higher, faster, than the election of another Trudeau to lead us ever deeper into the abyss, yet that's precisely what they've threatened us with.

Sheila's got Bubble trouble

May 31, 1999

If I were an Ontarian, I'd vote Conservative. Mike Harris hasn't done all things well, but at least he's had the fortitude to stand up to the unions and make some substantial, and, I believe in the end, positive changes to that province's environment.

In response to recent school shootings in Littleton and Taber, opposition leader Dalton McGuinty suggested hiring more psychologists and social workers to prevent a similar tragedy from occurring in his province. In typical liberal fashion, Mr. McGuinty would throw money he doesn't have at a problem in the hopes it goes away, seemingly unaware that that very propensity is at the root of many of our nation's woes. In good conscience I couldn't support anyone who chooses to represent the Liberal party regardless of jurisdiction. Harris would have my vote by default.

On the federal front the Liberals tax us and tax us and tax us and persist in throwing money at stupid projects, one of the latest being the lesbian porn flick, *Bubbles Galore* (1996). That production was financed by Liberal hack appointees on the Canada Council, Telefilm Canada and two tax-funded provincial organizations in Ontario. (I repeat, Harris has not done all things well.) It cost me and thee and Ontario taxpayers a total of $127,000 to bring this project to completion.

Canada Council falls under Sheila Copps' Heritage ministry. Copps pointed out that the grants were approved by hangers-on from the Mulroney era. In her defense she may have been mistaken, but *Bubbles* was in fact approved long after the last Mulroney appointees had been replaced by Liberal party faithful – the same lackeys who more recently approved yet another $60,000 for yet another lesbian barn burner, *The Girl Who Would be King.*

Why do they do this? To create wealth. The people involved in these productions would be that much poorer but for the public's intervention. What they overlook is that the public itself is that much poorer for the transaction. Left in the hands of them that earned it, the cash would produce far more economic benefits than when expropriated and flushed down the toilet on second rate films. So arguably they're not creating wealth, but destroying it.

Another reason to invest in Canada's film industry is to ensure its success, except that doesn't work either. By subsidizing any industry the government creates a welfare mentality within it. The need to produce quality goods for which people will pay is thereby diminished in proportion to the amount an industry is supported by other means (our taxes). For proof, I give you *Bubbles!*

UPDATE: I claimed above that I wouldn't vote Liberal in any jurisdiction, but that's not quite true. B.C. Liberal leader Christy Clark is cute and she's not NDP and... well, she's cute and she's not NDP! And that smile! I'm not totally shallow, but she had me at "hello."

And justice for none

June 14, 1999

Today an impaired charge causing death is punishable with a maximum sentence of fourteen years. Grit legislation tabled in May would see that increased to a life sentence. Reform, eager to look tough on crime, backs the bill. Of all groups, the Bloc stopped it from being fast-tracked through the Commons.

"We cannot be more severe for drunk drivers than serial killers," said MP Michel Gauthier. Paul Bernardo has been given one life sentence for the rape and murder of two school girls – Clifford Olson likewise for killing God only knows how many. Under this bill an otherwise law abiding citizen who had a few beer with his mates after work could end up in a cell next to either of the above for an equal period of incarceration. This is madness!

The same bill raises the maximum sentence for causing injury while driving impaired to ten years. There's a man in prison for multiple murder who's up for parole after ten years! In another case, a young man was sentenced to five and a half for cold blooded murder but could be out in as little as two on good behaviour.

The latter incident not surprisingly involves a native perpetrator on whom our judiciary has been instructed to go soft because of his disadvantaged background. Some have gotten away with murder; others have been sentenced to an extended camping trip to find themselves or get in touch with their roots or something.

For the record I'm not anti-native, but I'm all for equal treatment under the law. Currently a native could quite intentionally shank me (as in the afore-mentioned incident) and get little more than a slap on the wrist. If this bill passes and I accidentally kill that same native after having a few cold ones, I'm hooped. Hello, Paul!

People have beaten others to death, used drunken-ness to get the charges reduced and been paroled in two years! Under these proposed changes one could be sentenced to ten for simply injuring someone. Not to belittle the latter crime, but there's a raging disparity here. Drunk driving is indefensible obviously, but if one is drunk and murders, the weapon used, be it a lead pipe or a car, is not overly relevant to the deceased and should not be a factor in sentencing. Nor should a man's skin colour be used against him in a court of law. Ever. Full stop.

UPDATE: In the summer of '09 an acquaintance answered a 5:00 p.m. knock at the door only to get a knuckle sandwich right smack in the beak for his trou-bles. With the largest of three intruders then holding him at knife point, the others looted his home and left. When informed that the three men walking away from his home were native, the officer who took the call responded, and I quote, "Well, come in sometime and fill out a report."

So ten years after the Supreme Court decided to go soft on natives, assault and armed robbery by them doesn't even warrant dispatching a cruiser! American Supreme Court justice Samuel Chase: *"...where justice is not impartially administered to all;* where *property is insecure,* and the person is liable to violence *without redress by law,* the people are not free"[7] (emphasis added). The year was 1803, and if that's the standard, we are enslaved indeed.

Grits willing to oust God

June 21, 1999

A petition was organized by the Humanist Association of Canada urging some changes to our *Charter of Rights and Freedoms.* The organization seems to be satisfied with the vast majority of the document but opposes the clause which recognizes the "supremacy of God." They would change the offensive language to the "supremacy of intellectual freedom."

Openly gay MP Svend Robinson presented the petition, and the Liberal government refused to discount it despite Reform's efforts to get them to do so. What Robinson has probably never considered is that he arguably has the freedom to advocate said removal of 'God' from the public domain precisely because of our Judeo-Christian heritage. It's a fact that wherever Christianity has gone, freedom and a growth in individual rights have followed. Look at a map! The freest countries in the world are those that are, or were, Christian.

Consider, on the other hand, what would happen to Svend if he advocated the removal of any reference to Allah in a Muslim country's constitutional papers. You know as well as I that he wouldn't last a fortnight. In Canada, alternatively, he can advocate all kinds of nonsense from his perch in the House of Commons until he's defeated at the polls – and though its likely the most overused of clichés, I'd defend his right to continue doing so no matter that I always disagree with him.

That said, having the alphabetical symbols in our Constitution which together refer to Him who, I believe, made us, no more makes this a Christian or godly nation than does having an unread Bible in every home. A godly or Christian nation would be one the population of which could be largely defined as such, and we can't do that. Ours is very much a post-Christian multicultural society in which there are almost as many slight and significant variations of belief as there are people in it.

While on the subject of faith, I heard a cynic on the radio one day casting doubt on the story of Noah and the flood by stating that every people group in the world share the same "folklore." You might remember from Sunday school class that the flood recorded in the Book of Genesis preceded the attempted construction of the Tower of Babel, at the conclusion of which Noah's descendants were divided into different language groups before going off with those whom they could understand. That the descendants of those groups (that would be all of us if the story is true) point to a common ancestor who came through a great flood should surprise no one. Rather, I humbly suggest it points to the inspiration of... 'the Book'.

UPDATE: Politics is, in part, the art of compromise. Prior to the passage of the aforementioned Charter, for instance, concessions had to be made, among them one regarding the inclusion of the divine in the preamble. Trudeau thought the idea positively medieval but allowed the plebes their small victory. A presumably godless commie who in the author's view did his best to destroy this nation – is there any hope for such a man? Absolutely, but I'll have to come back to that.

A useless United Nations

August 10, 1998

The travesties of the Holocaust, Cambodia, the former Yugoslavia and Rwanda (to name but four examples) show clearly the depravity of the human heart. The latter three also serve to highlight the utter and complete uselessness of the United Nations.

Concerning Rwanda specifically, the CBC recently revealed that the UN could have easily prevented the genocide there and had in fact received many warnings of the impending disaster, yet repeatedly failed to respond. When violence did erupt, they didn't send in troops to suppress the poorly armed Hutu aggressors. Instead, believe it or not, they pulled them out leading to the wholesale slaughter of hundreds of thousands of defenseless Tutsies.

To his great credit Lt. Col. Romeo D'Allaire flatly disobeyed the order to withdraw, kept his troops on the ground and continued to protect those whom he could. Frankly the man deserves a medal for disobeying a direct order and doing what he knew to be the right thing. The UN, though, is not merely useless; it's positively detrimental to the public good.

At the time of this writing, UN member countries are in Rome negotiating the creation of an International Criminal Court (ICC). Although being set up under the auspices of trying war criminals, conservative observers view it as no less than a UN challenge to national sovereignty and an outright attack on jurisdictions which promote family values.

Although it will try war criminals, (a worthy objective indeed) according to legal experts this court will also, like no other body in history, promote the radical feminist agenda around the world. As an example, 'enforced pregnancy' is written into its statute as a transgression which would fall under its jurisdiction. Sounds reasonable, except this 'crime' has nothing to do with rape which is already addressed at the national level.

Rather, ICC delegates refer to 'enforced pregnancy' as the condition of any woman denied permission to abort a fetus at any stage of gestation and would sanction any government that denied or limited access to the procedure. So much for national autonomy in the UN's brave new world!

I referred to the UN as detrimental to the public good. My definition of public obviously includes the unborn, who, as human beings, (be they sentient or otherwise) should have every constitutional protection extended to them. Today in Canada a doctor can administer pre-natal surgery or death, depending on the wishes of a third party: the mother. It shouldn't be.

UPDATE: To ensure there is no misunderstanding, I believe the UN is a wine bibbing, hors d'oeuvre nibbling, tax sucking colossal farce. And my antipathy for the organization predates its rejection of our superior (but unlike Portugal's) non-China backed bid for a seat on the Security Council in 2010, and even its insistence that we save the world by committing 'cap and fraud' style economic suicide the year before that. (Wikileaks documents confirm that UN officials know that their carbon trading schemes are ineffective at everything except transferring wealth.) In fact it would be difficult to pinpoint precisely when my contempt for the organization galvanized, but its problems date right back to the day of its founding.

FDR's right-hand man, Alger Hiss, was instrumental in both the creation of the organization and the drafting of its original charter. Notably, he's also been proven sixty ways from Sunday to have been a spy on the payroll of one Joseph Stalin. That the UN provides diplomatic cover for terrorists and dictators today (a certain Gaddafi chairing a human rights commission comes to mind) should therefore surprise no one. It was indirectly created by one, so what would you expect?

Not satisfied with merely propping up dictatorships, the organization also seems determined to undermine the free. In 1976, Canada ratified the United Nations International Covenant on Economic, Social and Cultural Rights. This document recognized "the right of everyone to an adequate standard of living... including adequate food, clothing and housing, and to (a) continuous improvement in living conditions" (Art. 11).

The ridiculousness of a "continuous improvement in living conditions" aside, (where would that end?) no mention is made of individual effort or ability, leaving one to conclude that this pleasant outcome was to be arrived at naturally (or rather very unnaturally) through good old fashioned redistribution. And the problem with that, with apologies to Margaret Thatcher, is that you eventually run out of other people's money. Not surprisingly this most socialist of documents was signed by Canada's then resident commie, Pierre Elliot Trudeau. So the UN is for all appearances a commie inspired threat to free, capitalist societies everywhere that should be shown the door of all of them.

Speaking of good-byes, a lady once asked me to include something on Family Law in this country were I to go back into print. Having travelled the valley of divorce only once but lengthwise, I felt at least moderately qualified to address the subject. So are many others, of course, and the following experience is that of a composite, of which your author is but a small part.

To begin with, though divorce is obviously no fun for anyone, if you're a man in Canada and the above laws suddenly become pertinent to you, you have my deepest sympathies. The odds are not in your favour.

If, as reported, 94% of custody cases are decided in favor of one gender while the other is left paying taxes on child support payments to cover the mortgage on the judicial cottage, obviously something is up. But is the system actually biased against men?

Consider the actual case of a woman with a fistful of DUIs who abandoned her third husband and fourth child when she ran off to Newfoundland with her latest lover. She came back, sued for custody and, though it meant putting thousands of miles between a boy and a doting father who had no DUIs and had frankly done nothing wrong, won. So it would certainly seem so.

Now that man may or may not have been, but our composite man was indeed inclined to observe the age old tradition of warming his kids' butts when they misbehaved. In fact he maintains that he spanked his kids all of about ten times over their then combined twenty years of existence. Apparently it was a last resort, as if it mattered. On the last three of those occasions the children's mother phoned the authorities before suing him for sole custody and charging that the police had a history of responding to his residence. Access denied.

After a year of very limited access to his children the charges were thrown out of Chambers because a good portion of what he had been charged with (spanking what was then an eleven year old child) was perfectly legal, and otherwise there was no evidence of anything even remotely untoward. Access reinstated... or so he thought.

Our composite man was looking forward to his first full weekend with his kids in over a year when an organization oddly enough called Family Services basically put the boots to him. "They're a Gestapo" according to a retired nurse who observed the organization for years, and you'll soon see why she gave them that handle.

The charges were thrown out of Chambers for lack of evidence, recall, but Family Court, into which Family Services then hauled the accused, is an altogether different animal. Proof is irrelevant there; accusation and suspicion all that's required. After yet another six months of delays and separation from his children a judge of this esteemed court sentenced our derelict father to yet another six months of supervised access, which is of course all he'd known for a year and a half by that point.

Toward the end of that six month period, and closing in on two years of limited access to his children, the head of the local division of the Family Services department wanted the $80.00/hr supervision extended for yet another three months, at his expense, because he was not yet, at that time she felt, "sufficiently pacifistic."

She went to court to seek the extension. Unable to afford a lawyer he argued against it himself on the grounds that it was simply an extension of what was already an enormous injustice being perpetrated primarily against his children. It was a partial victory as she got only a one month extension, but as he soon discovered that old girl didn't like to lose at all and knew precisely how to get even.

A few hours later his cell phone rang. It was her, claiming he had expressed some anger in court that morning. Note: he'd been denied access to his children—and they to him—for two years, (ten hours of supervised access a month hardly counts) for what amounted to no more than some moderate discipline. If he wasn't angry he absolutely should have been!

He maintained, though, as he does to this day, that he didn't even so much as raise his voice in court that morning but had merely been direct and confident in his assertions. His protestations fell on deaf ears, of course, and she denied him ANY access to his children, supervised or not, for the balance of the extension. Frankly I think the woman should give thanks every night that he was "sufficiently pacifistic" to not go postal.

But maybe "Gestapo" is too harsh a judgment. Maybe, but of the eight hundred men between the ages of twenty-five and forty who commit suicide in Ontario every year, fully half are tied up in Family Law at the time of their demise, with people like her, and they're every bit as dead as if they'd been lined up in a ditch and shot. Of course if Family Services is a Gestapo, divorcing fathers would be what if not at the same time both their Jews and their meal ticket?

On a related issue, an acquaintance and his wife adopted two young siblings, both, it was later discovered, suffering from Fetal Alcohol Syndrome. They also discovered they were rather adept at raising them. Fifteen years later the boy (there was one of each) told his worker that he wasn't entirely happy living there. That being her highest priority she pulled him out. Eighteen months later he'd been in fifteen different homes and was then living under a bridge in Edmonton.

Another adoptive couple discovered they were also rather adept with high needs kids and purposefully adopted a couple with FAS issues. All went relatively well until the thirteen year old FAS daughter confided to her worker that her fourteen year old FAS brother had been molesting her. (She'd recently learned about sex.)

A psychiatrist confirmed the girl was prone to fabrication and nothing she said could be taken at face value. Add to this that she was never physically examined to determine the validity of her claim. Notwithstanding the above, the couple in question lost not only their adoptive children but their natural born family as well. And what do all these cases have in common?

Social workers. I tried to sell a book to a hooker one day who used to be one prior to Ralph's (mostly) misguided cutbacks. As both our sales approaches were unsuccessful, my only regret is not suggesting that she might actually be doing less harm to society in her current role. Of course I'm not suggesting there aren't some good social workers out there doing some meaningful, beneficent work, but do you really think we need an army of them running around every province telling parents how to raise their kids, disrupting families that aren't, in their view, sufficiently liberal?

On the matter of the helping professions, you will recall that our composite man spanked his kids most infrequently leading to some legal challenges. When he brought said infrequency to the attention of a psychologist then engaged in a home study, in his words she "near fell off her chair" having assumed from the allegations against him that it was more like a daily occurrence. Guess which easily substantiated fact she forgot to mention in her $11,000, forty-five page report!

When he had a good weekend with his kids it was credited to the supervision (with no evidence offered supporting a correlation); when his ex-wife demonstrably messed up, well, she was working on it. I'm not making this up. I read the report twice. He could have walked on water. It wouldn't have helped.

So again I ask: is the system biased against men? Overwhelmingly, obviously, and the only satisfactory solution in this layman's opinion is to enshrine in law, in the absence of mitigating circumstances, the concept of equal parenting following divorce.

In conclusion, is there any connection between the provincial department known as Family Services referred to in this update and the International Criminal Court of the preceding column? Only that both are manned by what are presumably well-intentioned people of a predominantly liberal persuasion who want the rest of us to think and live as they do, and who think nothing of using the full weight of the law to force us into line.

I refer to their good intentions not only to be generous but because in many cases it's probably very true. It's also true, of course, that the road to hell is paved with the very best of them, and it's just a hunch, but I suspect one day many lawyers, judges and meddling bureaucrats will wake up to find themselves at the wrong end of it.

Earlier you read that your author was but a small part of the composite referred to in this update. I lied; I am the composite. And why, you ask, would any of this, let alone all of it, happen to me specifically? Well, I can't answer that question with 100% certainty, (it is, after all, distinctly possible that I really am a bad egg) but I suspect it was because I wouldn't have believed any of it unless it did. Some things apparently have to be experienced first hand.

Secondly, and this is just a theory, but maybe Someone upstairs knew that this book just wouldn't be complete without an exposé on what is laughably called Family Services in this country, and maybe He allowed me to go through what I did because He knew that if my eyes were opened to this stuff—*and I was sufficiently provoked!*—I wouldn't shrink back from including it here. He did; they were; I was; and now I have. That's my theory anyway. It's the one that helps me make sense of this crazy world we live in.

Thanks for reading

September 14, 1998

Whatever the federal Liberals' purpose in promoting gun control legislation, it is not to reduce crime. In fact, examples abound of how legislation like Bill C-68 actually increases crime rates. Britain, for one, brought in gun control legislation in 1988 and robberies involving the use of firearms doubled in the intervening decade.

An American state which imposed similar legislation not surprisingly saw an increase in firearm related crime, except in the county that rebelled and passed a bylaw requiring all home owners to have a gun. Exceptions were made for every reason under the sun and the bylaw wasn't enforced, but the criminal element got the point and went elsewhere where they didn't feel so obviously threatened. Self-preservation is the name of that game.

Handguns have been restricted in Canada for seventy years so Bill C-68 is targeted at shotguns and rifles, again with the stated intention of reducing crime. What complete bunkum!

Stats Canada has shown that substantially less than 1% of all violent crimes involve long guns. Of all violent firearm related incidents, only 6.09% involve rifles or shotguns and approximately 75% involve handguns, 90% of which are owned illegally and will continue to be after C-68 is in place (it being a given that the criminal element will pay no more attention to gun registration laws than they do any other).

Liberals know that gun control laws increase crime, (they do read) but they'll continue to spout its reduction as their objective, false as it may be. One might conclude that their true objective is confiscation. Or maybe it's the UN's objective and our Liberals are just lackeys carrying out orders. This makes more sense as gun control is not merely a Canadian phenomenon but is happening in many parts of the world.

I was criticized a while back in this paper by an ex-serviceman (like me) for deriding the United Nations as ineffective and detrimental to the public good. I was in no way deprecating the sacrifices of servicemen and women who have fought in defensive wars or otherwise been involved in UN duties.

I was questioning the organization's ability to keep peace where there is no peace, (the former Yugoslavia) its cowardly withdrawal from Rwanda as attested to in a CBC news documentary, and its newly acquired taste for being a busybody in what are purely national affairs through the International Criminal Court. I am, though, encouraged that someone reads the column and cares enough to respond. Thanks.

UPDATE: I speculated above that the UN 'might' be behind the push for gun control legislation. In 2013, all doubt was removed when that organization passed the Arms Trade Treaty mandating that member countries track and record the sale of "conventional arms" – AND their "end users." (That would be you, Martha and Henry.)

They assure us, of course, that this won't lead to confis-cation, as did the Lieberals – right up 'till the day in 2005 when Paul Martin promised to solve the national gun crime crisis by confiscating all half-million registered, legally owned hand guns in this country. Had Martin's party survived the impending election and proceeded with this diabolical plan, his name would have merely been added to a long list of despots.

In fact fully nineteen times in the past century gun control legislation has been enforced somewhere on the globe, each time justified as an anti-crime measure despite, to the best of the author's knowledge, having never accomplished that objective. It is a simple fact of history, though, that every major genocide of the past century has been preceded by gun control legislation and confiscation. From the Armenian Turks in 1915 to the Jews in WWII Poland to the innocents in Pol Pot's killing fields of Cambodia the story is the same: registration, followed by confiscation, followed by slaughter.

Now Paul Martin is not Pol Pott, and Justin Trudeau presumably no Adolph Hitler, but they do belong to a political party that, much like their NDP brethren, seems to be tied at the hip to the UN. That, one might safely assume, is why the Liberals gave us Bill C-68 in the first place and why the NDP support it as if they birthed it themselves. So if I'm correct, voting Liberal or NDP is kind of like asking to be governed, albeit indirectly, by the UN itself. And if you're good with being governed even indirectly by an organization itself indirectly created by Joseph Stalin, then it's a safe bet you haven't read *The Gulag Archepelago* (1973), Alexander Solzhenitzen's personal account of life in a communist dictatorship. I calculate that if that book doesn't disabuse "useful idiots" of their infatuation with communism, nothing will… until they become its victim.

FURTHER UPDATE: Anastasia Desousa was murdered at Montreal's Dawson College with a small arsenal of registered weapons; thirty-two students were shot dead at Virginia Tech. What do these jurisdictions have in common? Restrictive, as opposed to liberal, gun laws, much like those the UN would impose on all of us if they could. The following column reveals what the author believes is really the only thing that might have reduced the carnage in these and other instances.

More guns, less crime

May 03, 1999

Mere words cannot describe the horror and revulsion evoked by the killing of twelve students and a teacher in a high school in Littleton, Colorado.

Shortly after this tragedy the CBC interviewed a fellow who bemoaned the fact that gun control legislation like that being implemented in Canada might have prevented it. Ralph Klein concurs, and despite being in an ongoing court challenge of the gun registry he says he's not actually against gun control: "We would support any laws—and those would be federal laws—that *strengthen* gun control." Odd words indeed from the man supposedly leading the charge against Canada's Bill C-68.

Unfortunately all the laws in the world couldn't prevent those little Hitlerites from obtaining all the weapons they wanted on the black market. Once the guns were in their possession, of course, the only thing that could have stopped them, realistically, would have been a responsible teacher with a weapon. In fact one recent U.S. school shooting was brought to a quick and nonviolent conclusion by just such an instructor.

Think: if just one woman in that ill-fated class at l'École Polytechnique in Montreal ten years ago had a little two-shot Derringer in her purse for personal protection, Marc Lepine might have been the only casualty that day. Guns, then, you must logically conclude, at least have the potential to save lives.

In his book *More Guns, Less Crime* (University of Chicago Press, 1998) law and economics professor John R. Lott Jr. makes the compelling argument that jurisdictions with the most liberal gun laws, as opposed to the most restrictive, are the safest. After studying over 3,000 counties in the U.S. over a sixteen year period he concludes that "allowing citizens to carry concealed handguns reduces violent crime, and the reductions coincide with the number of concealed handgun permits issued."

This makes perfect sense. Criminals are motivated, much like the rest of us, by self-preservation. The proliferation of handguns amongst a law abiding citizenry acts as a deterrent to the criminal element for the simple reason that they don't know who's carrying. And it works! In an eastern seaboard state that had recently passed such a law, a little old lady popped a thug and the crime rate in the area fell like a lead weight.

Obviously we can't bring back those who perished in Colorado or anywhere else for that matter, but governments can reduce the chances of these tragedies recurring by passing legislation that would permit the carrying of concealed weapons by qualified citizens. They won't. It's politically untenable in Canada today. That said, the drive to register, restrict and confiscate weapons in this country is clearly a move in the wrong direction.

UPDATE: Recall that the Alberta Tories for years claimed they opposed the billion dollar gun registry and would not prosecute its provisions. The feds can do their own dirty work, said they. Yada yada yada....

On the day the registration boondoggle came into effect, Oscar Lacombe carried an ancient, unregistered .22 rifle, without firing pin or bullets and double wrapped in plastic onto the grounds of the Alberta Legislature where he had served for a number of years as sergeant at arms protecting the politicians.

If charged by the feds, he would have had an opportunity to put the registry to a Charter challenge. It would be possible for the feds to avoid this, however, by having the province prosecute Mr. Lacombe under the criminal code over which it has jurisdiction.

Recall the Alberta Tories claimed all along they would not aid and abet the Liberals on this matter, so it seemed the challenge would be a go. That would have been the case if there were a shred of honesty in this government. Oscar Lacombe was in fact charged, under the criminal code, BY THE PROVINCIAL GOVERNMENT OF ALBERTA(!), the same people he used to defend. If Mr. Lacombe felt a cold, steel blade penetrating his back ribs, the man at the other end would be none other than Ralph Klein.

Like his gay rights charade, his support for familial autonomy and pretty much everything else he 'stood for', it's obvious that Klein's challenge of the gun registry was but a costly song and dance for the cameras. I suspect that, chest-thumping aside, like most liberals he probably wouldn't be content until we were all disarmed, save the police and criminals. But is that a remotely desirable outcome?

On October 22, 2014 a masked terrorist murdered Cpl. Nathan Cirillo who was ceremonially guarding the Tomb of the Unknown Soldier in our nation's capital. The terrorist was eventually killed by Sergeant-At-Arms Kevin Vickers. The difference between the living and the dead, of course, is that Mr. Vickers' weapon had bullets and a firing pin. Had Cpl. Cirillo enjoyed the same advantage, the day might have had a dramatically different outcome. And what, pray tell, if that recent convert to Islam had targeted Tim Hortons? Now is it time to reconsider our restrictive gun laws? If not, when?

Promote higher values (and bear arms?)

May 24, 1999

Three weeks ago this column dealt with the inverse relationship between levels of violent crime and the number of concealed gun permits issued in a given jurisdiction, and in which I tried to make the case for increasing the latter to reduce the former. Most, I presume, would oppose such a development in Canada. Fair enough. It's a free country, and people in it are still free to express their opinions – unless, of course, they're being interviewed by our left-wing national media and hold opinions with which they disagree.

Following the Littleton massacre, Valerie Pringle of Canada AM was yammering about the American right to bear arms and how this tragedy might have been averted if they only had gun control legislation like that which we enjoy in Canada. The father of one of the students disagreed, stating that he and his wife were in favour of Colorado's concealed weapons law and that the incident was not about guns but about a flaw in society which drives young men to violence.

He no sooner made the comment than he was cut-off, the scene reverting to the studio where Ms. Pringle and her cohorts berated him for his position. In typical liberal (cowardly) fashion, they were criticizing ideas opposed to their own without giving the author of those ideas an opportunity to defend them.

Obviously I concur with that father. Why? Because

there occasionally comes a time in some people's lives when they're either glad they had a gun or wish they did. Would you not have preferred one of the young women at the University of Montreal to have popped Marc Lepine before he got off a shot. Or one of the young men, rather than obey the order to leave the room? (Seriously, what choice did they have?) Should a woman about to be raped be able to defend herself, or would you suggest disarming her? Guns, in fact, where they are legal, diffuse many such potentially violent confrontations without ever being fired. Their presence alone accomplishes that purpose.

So how do we prevent Littleton or Montreal or Taber from recurring? We can't. Kids today are often growing up in a cultural wasteland. Parents in particular need to change that, but in the meantime it wouldn't hurt if responsible, qualified people could bear arms. The next time someone shoots up a school I'd want at least some of their teachers to be able to deal with the situation, and that means either carry concealed or open carry laws or both. There's no other way.

UPDATE: In the wee hours of Anno Domini, a man I will generously refer to as Herod the Nutjob slew all the children in Bethlehem and its surrounding environs two years of age and under, suspecting that among them was a challenger to his throne. And thus it was that "(a) voice was heard in Ramah, weeping and great mourning, Rachel weeping for her children, and she refused to be comforted, because they were no more" (Mat. 2:18, NASB). Sadly, in the closing days of 2012, in Newtown, CT, many more Rachels were created. Now obviously we can't legislate mental health, but we can protect our loved ones from the deranged, who continue to walk among us, by packing heat. Sadly, at the risk of repeating myself, I see no other way.

Two organizations I won't support

November 16, 1998

Like a good soldier I work, support local businesses when at all possible and pay my taxes. So I give the government their due, but unlike those who flush their paycheques down the government owned toilets known as VLTs, I don't look for ways to give them more from my limited pot.

One can go broke playing the slots in Vegas which pay out somewhere in the vicinity of 97%. One will obviously do so that much faster playing the Alberta bandits, widely known to pay out substantially less. Those who play them are apparently willing to shoulder more than their share of the provincial tax burden, and I won't be joining them anytime soon.

Nor will I give more support than I already do through my federal tax dollars to the United Nations. I can't stop the feds from playing heroes to the world by propping up the organization, but I can refuse to support UNICEF. It, merely an appendage of the UN, is rife with waste.

To quote David Frum, "More than 30% of the money you drop in the UNICEF box never leaves Canada. It's consumed in its ten Canadian offices – and the administrative costs here pale in comparison to those at its international HQ in New York." Every charitable organization has administrative costs. Although UNICEF's seem inordinately high, that's not why I don't support them.

I don't support UNICEF because I don't morally support its parent company, the UN, and the anti-family values that organization promotes. Promoting a woman's 'right' to terminate a pregnancy at will and at taxpayer's expense would be just one of them. But they do good work, you might argue. So does Hamas, I rebut (building schools and hospitals and such) and I won't support them either because of the other stuff they do!

Thankfully the kids in my neighbourhood weren't jingling any UNICEF boxes on Halloween night, thus saving me the trouble of having to explain all this to their innocent young minds. Stay tuned next week for one organization I consider it an honour to support.

ADDENDUM: This is a little out of place, but I promised earlier to return to the issue of a left-wing merger. In the 2011 election the Tories secured approximately 40% of the popular vote, the NDP 30% and the Liberals, twenty. Adding the NDP and Liberal numbers together would obviously spell disaster for the Tories, but that's an oversimplification. Many Liberals would rather eat dirt than join forces with the NDP, and vice versa, but the parties really aren't that far apart ideologically. Both want to increase taxes and benefits while cutting military spending... *just-like-the-Communist-Party-of-Canada.*

I put to you, therefore, that these three organizations are like trains running on parallel tracks: they move at different speeds, but they all eventually lead to the abyss. This is not to say the train we're on today is moving away from the abyss; it's just moving considerably slower than the others. To get the Conservatives to reverse course, though, we need to become more conservative ourselves – and that means educating ourselves. The author has a plan that might involve him getting filthy rich. If you instinctively recoil at the thought, it's a safe bet you're on the wrong train.

One organization I will support

November 23, 1998

It has been said that the freedom and prosperity we have experienced in Canada is directly related to the Judeo-Christian principles on which this country was founded. Why? Because the roots of the system of Tort law under which we operated until 1982 can be traced, through Rome, right back to the Ten Commandments.

That, of course, was the year Pierre Trudeau patriated the Constitution and as a bonus gave us *The Charter of Rights and Freedoms.* Besides limiting our freedoms by stating them, this document bequeathed unheard of powers on an appointed, unelected body of legislators known as the 'Court Party'. Not satisfied with just interpreting the Charter as written by our politicians, these judicial activists began 'reading in' words and phrases they felt should have been there in the first place. Unfortunately for those who disagree with this practice, we can't unelect those we haven't first elected.

One could be excused for throwing up one's hands in despair, but there is an answer. Brian Rushfeldt is the founder and head of the Canada Family Action Coalition, (CFAC) an organization that combats judicial activism and promotes the restoration of some of the principles on which this country was founded. One such area of philosophical confrontation is the court's blatant expansion of gay rights. One such battleground is Alberta. The judges, as my faithful readers know, have an ally in Ralph Klein.

After fighting the lower court's Vriend decision to the Supreme Court, Klein turned around and defended the higher court's decision to let the lower court's ruling stand, this in complete disregard of the thousands of Albertans who contacted him requesting he use the Notwithstanding Clause to opt out of the legislation.

Knowledge is power, and one of CFAC's objectives is to create a more informed electorate. People need to know not only how these decisions affect them but where the various candidates stand on issues, thus enabling them to make a more informed decision on election day. For more information you can call CFAC in Calgary at (403) 295-2159 or find them on the web at www.familyaction.org. Obviously I encourage it.

UPDATE: On the matter of judicial activism, a little known fact about the legal profession is the number of gay men within it. Compared to the general population it's virtually teeming with them according to a source in government. People need to be free to live their lives as they choose and choose their livelihoods obviously, but this all starts to add up when you realize that the push for gay marriage largely came from within the legal community itself. If you'll again follow the bouncing ball for a moment, the judges who made those pro-gay marriage decisions were appointed by arms-length boards, but before being considered for selection they first had to be elected from what is in effect a lawyers' union. When you consider its makeup then, it becomes apparent that those put forward for promotion to the bench have to first win what is in reality little more than a popularity contest in what increasingly looks like a gay bar. (Pun fully intended, of course.) Putting a cop on that board in '06, for which the Tories caught seemingly endless hell from the liberal media, was but a wee tiny baby step in the right direction.

Another one I won't support

January 11, 1999

In November I wrote about two organizations I refuse to support: the Alberta government which I won't lose to by plugging money into VLTs and the United Nations through their UNICEF campaign. Cold and heartless though I may seem, I had my reasons.

The following week I wrote about what in my estimation is the very worthy Canada Family Action Coalition which fights judicial activism and promotes the restoration of some of the principles on which this country was founded. I've unearthed another which decidedly is not.

Citizens for Public Justice is basically a group advocating public policy that hasn't the mind for it. I regret beginning to read their material at 10:30 PM as it cost me a good night's sleep of which I already get precious few (caffeine, not a guilty conscience, being the root cause – I think).

I was almost apoplectic when I read that "Governments could make a commitment to full employment by replacing many of the jobs eliminated in the public sector". Firstly, full employment, though seemingly desirable is not because it places too much power in the hands of the unions, ultimately driving up everyone's cost of living. Union leaders would love such a development; it's consumers who would be left wanting.

Secondly, big government bureaucracies are the driving force behind our unconscionable levels of taxation leading directly to lower investment and correspondingly higher levels of unemployment. CPJ's goal of full employment is not only misguided in the first place, but the method by which they aim to arrive there would assuredly produce starkly different results.

Another point of dissension is the organization's defense of the Supreme Court's Delgamuukwa ruling and their promotion of aboriginal self-government. This ruling establishes aboriginal title to huge tracts of land not covered under the original treaties and is a hugely irresponsible decision on the part of the Supremes.

Regarding self-government, A) we don't need to be supporting another level of bureaucracy and B) a majority of rank and file natives in fact voted against the same when they voted against the Charlottetown Accord. So arguably even they don't want it!

Citizens for Public Justice, as I wrote in the beginning, is in my view a public policy advocacy group without the mind for it. I can't imagine they're thinking through the policies they promote.

UPDATE: On the native file, one possible solution, which the author advances without prejudice, is to just pay them off. We're going to over time anyway. Why not take five to eight years of the Native Affairs budget, (fifty to eighty billion dollars today) and divide it up equally between qualifying natives in exchange for their signatures disqualifying them and their descendants from future entitlements other Canadians don't enjoy. They could pool their resources, buy Tim Hortons franchises clear across the country and live like kings, still on my nickel, but this time it would be a legitimate business enterprise. If I were a native looking around at the rez, I'd vote for it in a heartbeat.

Not your average identity crisis

December 12, 1998

Once upon a time I was proud to be Irish. I had no way of knowing it, but I imagined my forebears to be rebels against the English imperialist dogs whose only objectives seemed to be to exploit foreign labour and resources while expanding their empire and tax base. Perhaps my great, great, great grandfather fought alongside Rob Roy, the Irish freedom fighter immortalized in the movie of the same name. Be that as it may, a few things have happened of late to quench this pride in my Irish heritage.

Firstly I found out I'm not Irish. (That would do it.) Mother has done some digging in the family tree and found that the only Irish connection was an English implant in the northern province. Remember those imperialists I was telling you about? That's right; they're family now, and you can only vaguely imagine the identity crisis your scribe endured the day he learned of it.

So I'm not proud to be Irish anymore because I'm not Irish, but nor might I be today even if I were, not after Drumcree, Ballymoney and Omagh.

Drumcree would be home to the annual standoff between the Protestant Orangemen and the police over the Orangemen's right to flaunt a 300+ year old victory over the Catholics known as the Battle of the Boyne. That was a significant victory—it's why England isn't Catholic—but surely not one worth celebrating three centuries later, particularly when that celebration turns to bloodshed. It would be akin to English

Canadians marching through Quebec City every year to commemorate our victory on the Plains of Abraham. Hmmmmm....

Ballymoney was where the sectarian hatred between the two groups resulted in the fire bombing deaths of three children, brothers Richard, Mark and Jason Quinn. The loss of one child is about the hardest thing a parent will ever endure. The loss of three at one time is almost unimaginable. That the boys' parents were divorced is irrelevant. Their pain will be every bit as real as anyone else's. Possibly worse. Pray for them if you remember to.

The Omagh bombing in which twenty-eight were killed may or may not have been in retaliation for Ballymoney, but it was most certainly carried out to rock the peace process. I wish the peace process well, but what Ireland needs is not an accord but forgiveness. Peace will probably never come to the Emerald Island unless genuine forgiveness is extended and people in both camps let the past be the past. And for that they don't need more Catholicism or Protestantism – they need Christ Himself.

ADDENDUM: It has come to the author's attention that his father's mother's side of the family is about as Irish as the day is long, making him at least partially so again. (Nice!) As this does not materially affect the premise of this book it was determined to leave the column unedited, and pulling it altogether would have been unthinkable as the opening line of the next would make little sense without it....

The greatest Christmas present of all

December 21, 1998

Last week I concluded this column by saying, in effect, that the Irish don't need more religion but Christ Himself... as do you and I. That statement presupposes that God is. Other secrets of the universe may remain a mystery, but I'm long past questioning that one.

The alternative to this presupposition of God and the belief that the world around us is not an accident is the belief that we're monkey spawn and it's all an accident, a theory for which there remains precisely zero empirical evidence. That's why they call it a theory.

The Bible alternatively teaches that our universe is the result of intelligent design, and that we are merely responsible for managing our little corner of it. God may have created the man who became a drunk, for instance, and even the process of fermentation for that matter. And He may have even inspired the invention of the internal combustion engine, but He didn't combine them. That was a management decision.

This having been said, Christian history teaches that God does intervene in the affairs of men, and that intervention culminated in His appearance on the scene in a manger in Bethlehem some 2,000 years ago. That birth is the reason for the season, as they say, but if the baby in the manger is the only Jesus you know, I'm afraid you're missing the big picture.

He didn't come to merely be born or even to teach us how to live. He came to die, full stop. Ancient Israelites had been instructed to shed the blood of unblemished animals for the forgiveness of sin, not because of its efficacy, (it had none) but as a foreshadowing of what God was preparing to do in Christ, otherwise known as the Lamb of God. In His life and death Christ fulfilled many biblical prophesies regarding the coming Messiah, and I have it on good record that He'll take care of the rest when he returns for his church.

Are you part of it? This might be a little hard to grasp, but you become such not by attending church, but by inviting the Head of the church, Christ Himself, into your heart. He says of that vessel, "Behold, I stand at the door and knock" and awaits your response. You, of course, have the God-given freedom to disregard this information, but I suggest that you'll be immeasurably happier in the long run if you don't exercise it.

POST SCRIPT: Thankfully, Michel Trudeau did not 'disregard the information'. Hitchhiking in Winnipeg he was picked up by a pastor en route to an evening service to which he tagged along, there reportedly responding to the message and accepting Christ as his Lord and Saviour. That was three weeks before his tragic death in the mountains of British Columbia. The light in that dark period, if my information is correct, is that he got right with God first.

And so, I'm reliably informed, did his father on his deathbed, among Pierre's last words being "I'm going to see Michel." They say we'll be surprised at who we meet when we get to heaven, but Pierre Trudeau? Is God's grace that big? More than that, unless I'm entirely mistaken, it's big enough to cover the author's overflowing cup too. That's why they call it amazing.

Bomb Belgrade into submission

March 08, 1999

Late last year Serbian shock troops (it is widely assumed) slew 45 Kosovo-Albanians and left their bodies to rot in an open grave. Among the dead were a young woman and a twelve year old boy. "This is an atrocity of enormous proportions," said Canada's UN ambassador Robert Fowler. He might as well have shook his fist in the wind and declared that if they (presumably the Serbs) do this just ten more times, we're gonna' get mad!

Kosovars have been a suppressed minority in the former Yugoslavia for most of the last century as the Serbs have exploited their territory for its rich mines and cheap labour. In 1989, the Butcher of Belgrade Slobodan Milosovic imposed martial law on the region. Tens of thousands have since been jailed and tortured. It is he to whom NATO and UN officials are today recommending the Kosovars submit in a type of pseudo-autonomy. The Kosovars have properly told these do-gooders to get a life.

Some things are worth dying for, and freedom pretty much tops the list. The peacemakers want the oppressed to submit to a man who, according to the UN, has presided over the murder of 250,000 mainly Muslim civilians in Bosnia, the rape of 25,000 Muslim women and the creation of two million refugees in the former Yugoslavia. "They've even offered some blue berets to help maintain the so-called peace, perhaps the same ones who stood by while the Serbs slaughtered 9000

Muslim civilians in Sebrenicia" to quote Eric Margolis writing in the *Sun* media chain. In this NATO proffered scenario our boys would work alongside Milosovic's to prolong the oppression. "It would be like working with Hitler's brown shirts" to finish the quote.

I believe in peace. Unlike some I believe it's maintained through superior fire power. (Face it peaceniks, nothing deters war like the threat of retribution at the hands of a capable opponent.) That being the case, I have little but contempt for Alberta's most recently appointed senator and former nuclear disarmament activist, Doug Roche.

An ounce of prevention is worth a pound of cure, and the simple fact of the matter is that more military preparedness would have gone a long way in the recently disarmed Europe of the mid-thirties. And like conventional weapons then, nukes are an obvious and essential deterrent today. Granted, there may well come a day when we can just sit around, sing Kumbaya and beat our swords into plowshares, but to do so while our enemies are beating theirs into bigger, more powerful swords is just plain nuts. In light of this, I believe Roche and his ilk are every bit as wrong-headed as their predecessors.

Margolis again: "NATO should not be in the business of repressing legitimate demands for independence and self-determination." What they should do is what they should have done when Serbia first invaded Croatia in the fall of 1990. Your humble scribe's recommendation heads the column.

UPDATE: Regardless of what you think of war, it's brought an end to slavery, Nazism, fascism and communism in some parts, to name just a few undesirable conditions. If you enjoy not living under them you have a vet to thank and a soldier to support.

Pacifists deeply misguided

April 19, 1999

Some are opposed to war period, and specifically today to NATO's acts of aggression in the former Yugoslavia. They're pacifists, they argue it's wrong for the rest of us to intervene in the affairs of a sovereign country, and they couldn't be more wrong.

If English Canada were to bomb, burn, murder or otherwise cleanse this country of its French speaking population we would understandably be condemned in the court of world opinion. Would it then be right for that world to just sit idly by and watch it happen? Of course not! We would expect intervention and the protection of innocents. Anything less would amount to acquiescence and be the moral equivalent of collaboration. That it took the world community so long to respond to the situation in the Balkans is frankly reprehensible.

"But people will be killed," the pacifists argue. People are being killed with or without military intervention, and those who argue against it frankly argue against history. The bombing of Hiroshima and Nagasaki caused inestimable damage and suffering, for instance, but so did the war which those bombs brought to an end, and it's undeniable that many American lives were saved by that government's use of superior fire power.

Pacifists believe that one can negotiate with devils. Again they argue with history, Hitler having entered into pacts of nonaggression with just about every country he shortly thereafter invaded.

And why did he invade them? Because he knew he could beat the tar out of them after the relative success of that era's peaceniks in disarming the western democracies. Do you not see then that the peaceniks themselves were in part responsible for the carnage of the Second World War?

Pacifists are almost invariably from the left of the political spectrum. Those on the right seem more acutely aware of the condition of the human heart and the depths to which it can plumb. In light of this, they're aware too that war is sometimes simply unavoidable. I humbly suggest that those who believe otherwise clearly do not well understand human nature.

UPDATE: While on the subject of peaceniks, Margaret Atwood, Naomi Klein, self-described "former" Marxist Judy Rebick and then socialist MP Svend Robinson issued a letter in 2002 declaring that war with Iraq would be immoral because it was "unprovoked."

Unprovoked. Saddam Hussein bombed several neighbouring countries, gassed tens of thousands of his own countrymen and was before his ouster both a financier and provocateur of terrorism. According to a physicist formerly in his employ, he was also actively pursuing an agenda of nuclear and biological weaponry development. That's what was known in 2002.

Foreign policy is not an exact science. It's based on other countries' leaders' histories and capabilities, neither of Hussein's having done anything to endear him to anyone. He was a terrorist and a thug, and there was the very real possibility that he had some hardware with which to deliver his spite.

What we now know, according to one General Georges Sada, Vice Marshall of the Iraqi Air Force and onetime Hussein advisor, is that it took fifty-six sorties of jumbo jet flights to hide the country's stockpile of chemical, biological and nuclear materials in Syria in advance of the first Gulf War.[8] Then sanctioned by Oil for Food which was none too effective, he thereafter continued to invest multiplied millions in advancing his nuclear ambitions. In light of all this it would have been irresponsible for junior to have *not* invaded the country.

While on the subject of foreign policy, what does Canada's experience in Afghanistan, America's in Iraq and Israel's ongoing conflict with its neighbours all have in common? Only that we were/are fighting what appear to be deeply misguided zealots with no regard for human life and Hitleresque ambitions of world dominion.

Civilians have, of course, been killed in each of these theatres. It is a fact that no army has yet devised a method of warfare that completely avoids civilian casualties, though minimizing the scale of such is the objective of at least the remotely civilized ones. This objective becomes increasingly difficult when one side in a conflict specifically targets civilian populations while using yet others as human shields, both in direct violation of the Geneva Convention. I'm referring now, of course, to both Hezbollah and Hamas, and no less a reliable source than their own *Al-Jazeera* newscast has confirmed their tactics.

In 2006, Hezbollah killed eight and kidnapped two Israeli soldiers in direct contravention of Geneva. By 2009, Hamas had fired no less than 7,000 rockets over a three year period on the Jewish homeland. In 2012, over a six day period, they launched a thousand more, killing five. In each of these cases Israel has provided a very measured response, (measured, as evidenced by the fact that Gaza and Lebanon weren't reduced to smoldering ruins) but anyone who questions what precipitated these actions is guilty of willful blindness.

In Gaza, Lebanon, and on the high seas Israel's actions have been entirely defensible – as they will be again when they get around to addressing the threat posed by the murderous Iranian regime's nuclear program (assuming they haven't done so before this goes to print.)

Defensible, and entirely justified – just like America when it went into Afghanistan to root out the perpetrators of 9/11, and as were we in our efforts to keep it from falling back into the hands of the terrorists. Girls are going to school today and their mothers are providing for their own through businesses started up with micro-loans. The Taliban, alternatively, would murder the girls for trying to get an education (✓) and sell their mothers into slavery to pay their debts. The left, marching in the streets with their tiresome "Troops Out Now" nonsense, as usual, knew not what they called for.

Nor, though, did anyone (save the military industrial-complex) want this to become another twenty-five year engagement like Cypress. At some point the country had to be turned over to the locals. As did Iraq at some point. Or did they? The rise of ISIS in 2014, and that group's unspeakable atrocities committed against both Christians and their fellow Muslims, leads one to question whether we can ever entirely leave that part of the world. But on the question of the timing of our withdrawal, there's one group the government should never listen to.

In June a Gallup poll revealed that 25% of Americans wanted their troops brought home from theatre. That was five months before Germany unconditionally surrendered to the Allies! The year was 1945. I'm referring to peaceniks, of course, and all one can say is thank God for the politicians who ignore them, both past and present.

It's all about faith

May 17, 1999

Joseph Riordon was laid to rest two weeks ago. He was a 45 year old Canadian military veteran who suffered from what many refer to as Gulf War syndrome. Symptoms were numerous and debilitating, and toward the end he was confined to a wheelchair as he could no longer walk without falling.

The military dismisses all such complaints as psychosomatic in an obvious attempt to protect themselves from liability. Those who suffer from it are acutely aware that it is very real and likely related to a bad batch of anthrax vaccine some of our servicemen reportedly received before heading to the Gulf in '91. Your humble scribe, in fact, might well have been among them.

After serving in the forces for eight years I gleaned from the author of the Book of Wisdom that it is God's gift that a man enjoy not only the fruit of his labours but even those labours themselves. Being miserable in my work and knowing there had to be something better I submitted my request for release the next day, as it turned out ten days before Saddam Hussein invaded Kuwait. Had I not you likely wouldn't be reading this column today as military service and political columnizing simply don't mix – and who's to say I wouldn't have long ago succumbed to the effects of that vaccine?

After five years of selling insurance an opportunity arose to work for the Canadian Taxpayers Federation and help that organization continue to influence public policy. Not knowing whether I'd sink or swim I stepped out in faith, shakily confident that my needs would be met. They were, but alas it's time not for another step but a small leap.

The Taxpayers are doing a good work, but my first priority, politically, is to bring down the Tory government in Alberta. This the CTF won't do, but the Social Credit Party might and it's to them I go as a fund-raiser. The fly in the ointment is that they have no money with which to pay me, so my economic survival will depend on being able to quickly reverse that situation. If I can't it would seem I've erred large, but steps of faith have thus far landed your scribe on solid ground. I suspect they'll do so again.

UPDATE: So was the fund-raising successful? Thankfully no, considering the party booted my charming personality out the door a few years hence. Having left the Taxpayers, though, set me on a journey leading to the publication of the first edition of this book and to the discovery that I had a bit of a knack for selling it door to door. The money raised kept your humble scribe in groceries, but the contacts made financed his now nine failed election campaigns. (Never say die.)

Note that 1) Winston Churchill, who financed his early campaigns through the sale of his books, lost five elections. 2) Abe Lincoln lost eight. 3) I beat them both! 4) The founder of People's Jewelers began by hawking his wares door to door during the Great Depression, and 5) this isn't People's Jewelers. Not yet anyway, but in the immortal words of Tom Hanks in the closing scenes of *Castaway* (2000), "I know what I've gotta do. I've gotta keep breathing, because tomorrow, the sun will rise, and who knows what the tide could bring in." It's still very much all about faith.

Taxation: For Good and Evil

August 09, 1999

Taxation is a force that can build, shape, and/or destroy civilizations. Rome is a fine example. Its thousand year history can be divided into two periods.

During the first, called the Republic, the Senate was in charge. This was followed by the period of the Caesars. The empire finally ended when it was sacked by the Vandals in A.D. 476. Some believe taxes contributed to its demise as much as any invading army.

Early Rome taxed its citizens lightly and their pragmatic policies were extended to their newly acquired colonies. And thus the state prospered. As the superpower's borders expanded, though, so too did its military and the taxes required to support the same. Increased expenditures on both that and an expanding bureaucracy brought about increasing financial pressures leading to excessive tax increases, evasion and the eventual bankruptcy of the state. Evidence of crippling levels of taxation prior to its fall has led some historians to believe that Rome simply taxed itself to death.

It was said by a sixteenth century historian, "The sun never sets on the dominion of the king of Spain and at the slightest movement of that nation the whole world trembles." A hundred years later it was reduced to a mere shadow of its former self, humbled not by invading armies but by the withdrawal of support from its own taxpayers. In response to what they perceived as extortionary tax rates, the Spaniards who didn't resort to violence took flight in every direction, effectively causing Spain to disintegrate for lack of revenue.

Eighteenth century France was characterized by inequitable tax laws which exempted the nobles and tax collectors and placed almost the entire tax burden on the shoulders of the peasantry. Taxes on peasant owned land, for example, were five times that on noble land. The guillotine bound nobles argued this made the peasants want to work harder to stay ahead of the tax man. Your scribe just about fell off his chair when Finance Minister John Manley said almost exactly the same thing one day!

It's said that people who won't learn from the mistakes of history are bound to repeat them. I suspect our politicians should have studied it—history, that is—rather than law. Just a thought.

UPDATE: Never entirely satisfied with this column, the author well knew that there was more to the fall of Rome than taxes and an invading army. There was also what in a less enlightened era would have been referred to as almost unprecedented moral decay in the land.

Now whether these things are related or not you decide, but would not verifiably rampant levels of homosexuality in latter-day Rome, corresponding as that would with a declining birth rate, also logically contribute to higher levels of taxation on a diminishing population? Obviously! In conclusion then, it would appear that the morally decadent Rome, yes, taxed itself to death – at least in part as a result of said decadence. Do you think just maybe there's a lesson in there somewhere for the rest of us?

Taxation: For Good and Evil, part II

August 16, 1999

Last week I wrote about how tax policies have shaped history and both built and destroyed nations. Space did not permit me to deal with the Netherlands. In the seventeenth century, Holland was in fact 'the' world superpower. It was short lived.

The United Provinces of the Netherlands came into being as a result of a tax revolt against the Spaniards (see last week's column) and proceeded a mere century later to fade from its superpower status as a result of its enormous military expenditures and high tax policies. In *The Dutch Republic,* (McGraw-Hill, 1968) Charles Wilson writes that "War meant expense (and) taxation. Taxation meant the strangling of trade." The Dutch Republic didn't collapse so much as decline, much like Spain before it and the British Empire after it, from the burdens of excessive taxation, debt and military expenditures wildly beyond its means.

While Holland was enjoying superpower status, Queen Elizabeth I (through an albeit circuitous manner) inherited a bankrupt England from her father, King Henry VIII. Instead of increasing revenues to match the demands of government, good Queen Bess reduced government to match existing revenues. As a result her subjects enjoyed the lowest taxes in all of Europe. Low taxes led to compliance and expanded immigration and investment. And thus, through wise tax policies, the

England she left to future monarchs was well on its way to becoming a superpower.

Canada has a tiny military to support compared to the nations referred to—the Liberals have made sure of that—but we are forced to finance one of the largest per capita bureaucracies in history – a veritable army of civil servants. In fact, it became laughably large during the Trudeau years. And successive governments instead of dealing with the situation have succumbed to, among other things, the power of the unions.

The provinces have fared no better with Alberta leading the way with the largest per capita government in the country. We enjoy the lowest tax rates in Canada not because of thrift and good governance but resource revenues. Full stop.

ADDENDUM: England's above mentioned superpower status has come and gone obviously, and there were many reasons for its decline, but the election of a succession of socialist (Labour) governments in the 20th century left the mother of parliamentary democracies "the sick man of Europe" in grave need of a saviour. Her name was Margaret Thatcher, her critics called her "Attilla the Hen," but the fact is that England's every economic indicator was in the loo when Maggie came to power in '79, and as a public servant (as opposed to a socialist idealogue masquerading as such) the job fell to her to reverse those trends. And thus the "Iron Lady" set her course, she was "not for turning" and the England she left to her successors was a healthier patient on every front. As a nominally political friend once said, "She was the best thing that ever happened to that country – and her own party kicked her out!" In the long annals of dumb things governments have done, that one simply has to take the cake.

We are a study of bad taxation

August 23, 1999

A heavy tax burden does not a great nation build. In fact at a certain point, higher rates of taxation actually generate lower revenues. This truism is illustrated on what's called a Laffer curve created by economist Arthur Laffer at the University of Southern California.

He further shows that there are two rates of tax that produce the same amount of revenue: one high, one low. The low rate stimulates economic growth and job creation, while the high rate naturally leaves less for private investment leading to economic stagnation. It's not rocket science; it's high school math.

The U.S. learned this the hard way when it hiked progressive income tax rates from 7% in 1916 to 77% in 1921. Revenues went virtually unchanged, but the number of filers dropped by 80%. Americans aren't stupid. Facing oppressive rates they fled for more friendly environs, as are many Canadians today in what's called the 'brain drain' in which many educated people with higher than average earning potential are fleeing our tax-and-spend governments.

Adam Smith in his great classic, *The Wealth of Nations* (1776), highlights four marks of a bad tax system. A tax is bad which 1) requires a large bureaucracy to administer, 2) obstructs the industry of the people, ultimately diminishing their ability to pay, 3) encourages evasion and 4) puts people through "odious examinations of tax gatherers and exposes them to much unnecessary trouble, vexation and oppression." With Canada's high marginal tax rates encouraging evasion, the GST police combing through the books for missing shekels and numerous payroll and hidden taxes, I suspect ours qualifies.

Taxes need to be paid if we're going to live in any kind of a country obviously, but equally obviously the more equitable and fair the taxes, the better the country. And how does ours stack up? When other countries send their finance ministers here to study how our government manages to fleece us to the degree that it does, without causing an armed revolt, you just know there has to be room for improvement.

UPDATE: There's room for improvement, granted, but so too things could get a lot worse if we're not careful. In the 2004 Ukraine election, exit polls showed reformer Victor Yuschenko with a commanding 10% lead. According to a story carried in *The Washington Post,* (May 1, 2005) the government fraudulently reversed the results and state-run television announced Yuschenko's defeat. A woman translated the message in sign for the hearing impaired. Or at least she was supposed to. At obvious personal risk she silently informed her viewers that the government was lying and Yuschenko was their president. And thus the Orange Revolution began, inspired by the bravery of a young woman raised by deaf-mute parents.

That Orange Revolution was an example of a country fleeing communism. Ours, in 2011, concentrated in Quebec though it was, basically amounted to flirtation with it. Obviously the author is satisfied with the Liberals' near annihilation in that election. That the tax-and-spend, money-grows-on-trees NDP became the government-in-waiting, though, should terrify Canadians. If you don't understand why, it would seem you need to read better books. Obviously I'm not getting through to you.

The good, the bad and the ugly

August 30, 1999

History is replete with examples of good and bad leaders. Queen Elizabeth I was a fabulous monarch who said, "It is not given to man to tax and be loved." One would presume what she meant was that a ruler cannot tax excessively and be respected by his or her subjects. She practiced what she preached, taxed modestly and was adored by her nation.

Peter the Great was a Russian Czar who followed a long line of incompetent leaders. He abolished the plow tax and the household tax which together had been crippling the economy and replaced them with a simple and single poll tax on all males. Peasants who worked hard and purchased new equipment and lands could keep the extra revenues generated. He reversed the declining Russian economy (albeit temporarily) by remaking the tax system, stimulating economic growth and decentralizing the state.

On a personal note, ladies, he was not the kind of guy you'd want to bring home to mother. Eating with his fingers, belching and flatulating in public, he was a bit of a boor. If his women wouldn't drink with him he would hold their noses and pour liquor down their throats. (I, by comparison, am a gentleman, just so you know.)

William Tell is famed in Switzerland not for shooting an apple off his son's head, but for inciting a successful tax revolt against Austria's King Rudolph. In 1315, Rudolph's troops descended on the Swiss infantry outnumbering them almost 10:1 and were still defeated! Apparently the Swiss were stronger mad than the Austrians were greedy.

There have been the good, the bad and the ugly in leadership throughout history, modern Canadiana being replete with the bad. In the '70s the Liberals gave us such an enormous per capita bureaucracy it was laughable on the world stage, and Trudeau himself will forever be remembered as the godfather of deficit financing.

Despite Brian Mulroney's '84 campaign promise to give civil servants "pink slips and running shoes," like a good liberal he hired a whack more and gave us the GST. As Margaret Thatcher noted in her memoirs, he was a Progressive Conservative who placed far too much emphasis on the adjective.

Many thanks to Charles Adams, author of *For Good and Evil: The Impact of Taxes on the Course of Civilization,* (Madison Books, 1993) for many of the facts and ideas presented in these last four columns. It's been an invaluable resource.

Gone truckin'

September 06, 1999

You may have noticed this column of late has been about historical issues as opposed to current events. In June your scribe found himself out of any meaningfully paying work, gave the editor of this publication a fistful of columns and headed out to seek his fortune in other parts. He made it to Toronto briefly, but ultimately the appeal of some good home cooked meals in Winnipeg won the day.

Over the summer, 'gun related crime' has become the new phrase on the lips of U.S. gun control advocates and politicians. Rather than gun control, perhaps they should follow Virginia's lead and introduce mandatory hard time for gun related offenses. There, if you're caught breaking the law with a firearm, the lesser charges are dropped and you're doing five years in the big house for the weapon. In Virginia they got tough on gun related crime and—big surprise—homicides dropped by 50%.

Back on Canadian soil polls are showing Reform languishing at four percent in Ontario while the Tories are hovering around thirty. The battle is for second place, but Joe Who seems to be winning the hearts and minds of central Canadians – and frankly my patience weareth thin. If after the next election we continue to have a Liberal government in Ottawa and Reform is once again beaten back into the hinterland, I'll be sorely tempted to champion the cause of western independence. I'm not a rabid separatist per se, but liberal governance that isn't worth a bucket of warm spit does make the concept look increasingly palatable.

On a subject of more immediate concern, do you remember Maslow's Hierchy of Needs? It's a pyramid, the base of which represents our primary needs of food and shelter and such. The pinnacle, if memory serves, is something called self-actualization. One must satisfy one level before moving on to the next. Somewhere in the middle, I presume, are things like writing a column. Through what history may judge as some less than astute moves I've been pushed hard to the base of the pyramid and can no longer devote the time required to write this one. Sadly, this will be my last.

For my next act I'll be seeing the world from the lofty heights of an 18 wheeler as I haul it across the continent to keep the wolf away from the door. Unfortunately I'll have little time for much else.

In closing, I hope you've enjoyed reading this column half as much as I've enjoyed writing it. I sincerely thank you who have faithfully done so this past year and a half. Your comments, both favourable and otherwise, have also been appreciated.

In conclusion, God bless. May you prosper and be in good health as your soul prospers... and may our paths cross again soon.

Fix Canada

Conclusion

Fix Canada

Conclusion

So what did your humble scribe do that history might deem 'less than astute', as recorded in the last column? I mentioned it a few pages back, but specifically I was referring to that fund raising effort that went south.

To quote a philosopher friend, "Things don't always work out the way we planned, but they always work out." That failure led to a short trucking career during which I saw some sights I'll never see again, (two of them having been flattened by jet liners) followed by the landing of a somewhat lucrative sales job, the proceeds of which financed the publication of the first of these books. I hope you've not been entirely disappointed with the outcome.

I'll expend only a little more ink on them here, but you will agree that I rode the Alberta Tories pretty hard in the early columns. I hope you will also agree that they deserved it! Granted, they temporarily balanced the budget and paid off the debt, but as I've argued in these pages anyone who couldn't do at least what that gang did in this resource-rich province, in that era, should probably be institutionalized.

Besides having the youngest, most labouring population in Canada, the Tories also benefitted from the triple whammy of having a lower level of government on which to download costs, (which they took full advantage of) from astronomical resource revenues they had little to do with and from almost unprecedented low interest rates. And despite having all this going for them, not only did they never balance a budget in the nineties without raising taxes as repeatedly claimed, they've also been behind two of the largest tax increases Albertans and Canadians have ever seen.

Until the first publication of this book in 2000, Alberta's provincial income taxes had been tied to the federal rate. Every boost in it thus led to a proportional hike in the province, so Klein's claim to have ever balanced a budget without raising taxes is blatantly false. Because of the way the system was rigged he was able to reap the benefits of tax increases without taking the heat for having introduced them. Not coincidentally, it was when federal rates started to decline that he chose to unhook from them.

To add salt to the taxpayers' many wounds, he was also responsible for two of the largest tax increases this province and nation have ever seen. As a result of forcing local councils to adopt the system of market value assessment in regard to property taxes, some folks in Alberta have been driven from their homes, gratis the man of the people.

The largest tax hike in all of Canadian history, though, has been the near doubling of the Canada Pension Plan premiums from 5.85 to 9.9% of a person's gross earnings, with a maximum contribution of $3500 per annum.

Why the limit? Simply and only to protect the wealthy from its effects. Under this legislation the struggling, self-employed individual earning $35,000 per annum or less will be required to fork over nearly 10% of his or her gross income to prop up what many believe is an unsustainable plan. The $70,000 earner, because of the cap, would contribute just under 5%. The $140,000 per annum individual, 2.5 and so on. Million dollar men like the Martin/Chretien team that gave it to us won't feel the pinch at all, but they didn't act alone. Klein's fingerprints were all over the thing.

To push it through, then federal Finance Minister Paul Martin required the support of two western premiers and Ontario's Mike Harris. He got the western support he needed from Gary Filmon and Ralph Klein, but Harris held out – until Klein took him aside and helped him see the light. And thus every working Canadian will be poorer because of Klein's corroboration with the federal Liberals on this issue. As this goes to print the feds are looking at making further changes to the plan. The only change that would be fair to the poor (and didn't someone once say we should always remember them?) would be to lower the rates and lift the cap.

The Alberta Tories deregulated power to the clear benefit of providers, they lined the pockets of the American packers during the BSE crisis and they've been selling off the black gold for a penny on the dollar. Your humble scribe admits zero expertise in any of these areas—and there's more to each than meets the eye—but if the Tories aren't shills for the multinationals he has no idea what one would look like.

This is not to say the positions enumerated above are all, necessarily, wrong. The Deutsche Bank rates the oilsands, for instance, as "bottom of the pack" amongst global energy projects competing for investment dollars. And that was after the major players invested billions developing the technology to turn the dirty sand into something marketable, and before the Tories decided to raise royalties $1.4 billion (since repealed) on the eve of an election in 2008. The industry was headed for a bruising anyway given the then soon declining price of that commodity, but the Tories exacerbated its problems for purely political reasons. That disaster was Premier Ed Stelmach's responsibility.

Ed stepped down in 2011. His replacement was a former human rights lawyer, UN bureaucrat and long-time Joe Clark booster named Alison Redford. Apparently a more liberal candidate couldn't be found, but have the Tories ever provided the province with remotely conservative governance?

According to Alberta's Public Accounts, on the day the province's first 'Conservative' premier Peter Lougheed left office, gross expenditures in Wild Rose country were fully eighteen times what they were the day he took office. Eighteen times! Adjusted for inflation, naturally. Don Getty went on to epitomize irresponsibility in the name of diversification, and Ralph Klein's cutbacks were grossly misdirected as explained in these pages.

And then there was Ed, who took it upon himself to chase our primary industry from the province, and Alison for whom the word 'entitlement' would have had to have been invented if it didn't already exist. Her replacement, Jim Prentice, is a red Tory who came out early and strongly for gay marriage, the likely long-term effects of which I will address shortly.

So the Tories in Alberta have always been liberal. If that message has been clearly communicated, mission accomplished. Or at least the smaller part of it.

An arguably more important objective has been to point out to eastern and central Canadians in particular just how very inadequate are the liberal governments they have, until recently, repeatedly returned to power.

Liberal parties, including the Liberals themselves, the NDP and the now defunct Progressive Conservatives, can take responsibility for our debt, the tax levels we bear, the unfunded liability in the Canada Pension Plan, our underfunded military, low productivity... the list is probably endless.

The PCs are history, of course, and the Liberals were thankfully reduced to rump status in the same 2011 election that gave the Conservative Party of Canada what will hopefully be the first of many majority mandates. This is not to imply that party isn't due its share of criticism after almost a decade in power. -

There is the small issue of the two broken promises to 1) not incorporate resource revenues in the equalization formula, (a promise half broken) and 2) to not tax income trusts, neither of which the author likes, but keep in mind there is a world of difference between making promises circumstances dictate you cannot keep (which is arguably the case here) and making those you have no intention of keeping. (GST anyone?)

Gay nuptials continue unabated. The author maintains this is arguably the most destructive social development in Canadian history. Why? Because as even its advocates will agree, gay marriage is a huge step toward the complete normalization of the homosexual lifestyle. As common sense dictates, the more mainstream homosexuality becomes, the more our youth will feel at liberty to experiment with it, thus becoming addicted to the lifestyle. Is that what we see unfolding today?

Consider that in 2009, 2% of the population self-identified as homosexual according to Stats Canada. In 2012, that number had increased to 5% according to a Forum Research poll, a 150% increase in three years assuming these numbers are correct. Obviously we're faced with the thorny issue of causation, (just because B follows A does not imply that A caused B) but in light of the equally obvious possibility of a correlation between these facts, and that we're talking about what is in reality an existential threat here, (remember Rome?) then gay marriage should frankly be kiboshed without delay. But how did we get to this point?

You will recall that I made much, earlier, about a possible correlation between the Kremlin and the evolution of gay rights in this country. Of course you understand that communists aren't that... provincial.

In *The Naked Communist,* (Ensign Publishing Co., 1958) author and former FBI agent Cleon Skousen outlined the agenda of the American Communist Party (CPUSA). This was, in part, to both eliminate prayer and dumb down the curriculum in the public school system; to promote environmentalism as a means of tying up business in red tape; and to promote cohabitation and homosexuality as "normal, natural and healthy." This not surprisingly coincided perfectly with the communist agenda espoused by party spokespersons at a '92 University of California Berkeley meeting attended by then future congressman Curtis Bowers, but back to Canada.

Today our public schools graduate functional illiterates who don't know the first line of the Lord's prayer, environmentalism is the new religion and cohabitation the new norm. And gay marriage is a reality in 2014 in nineteen countries, all of them democracies, none communist.

Are communists responsible for all of these developments? I don't know. I told you, I'm just a layman. But I can add, and that communists infiltrate democracies to mess them up is yet another long established fact, so I reckon it's a distinct possibility. But what can be done about it?

Well, "The first thing we do," to quote Dick the butcher in Shakespeare's *Henry the Sixth,* "let's kill all the lawyers." Or better yet, let's just destroy their handiwork, as mentioned, by kiboshing gay marriage. And while we're at it we can euthanize Trudeau's Trojan Horse by shredding the Charter that led to it, thus making our elected representatives (and ultimately us, for we elected them) once again supreme.

And then we can shut down the Supreme Court that rammed gay marriage down our throats in the first place. That freedom of speech hating body was created by an act of parliament in 1875 and can be unmade in precisely the same manner.[9] And while we're at it we can re-write our mixed-up, self-conflicting constitution to better reflect our values. (Or better yet, looking around, those of our founders, assuming we can remember them.)

What's that? It can't be done? Why then did Liberal leadership candidate Michael Ignatieff recommend a constitutional do-over in 2006? In fact all of the above can be done, but what we need to bring these things about is a conservative government, a small group of politicians with their heads screwed on right and Thatcheresque resolve to withstand the beating the left will inevitably lay on them. That the Tories haven't taken any noticeable steps in this direction as this goes to print is frankly disappointing.

Now to give credit where credit is due, the Tories did well by raising the spousal exemption to the level of the personal exemption in the 2007 budget, (thus eliminating what was in reality a 'marriage penalty') as well as granting families a $2000 per child tax credit. Pro-family is all good. The announcement of personal tax cuts along the way have been equally welcome. The reduction in corporate income tax to the economic tiger neighbourhood of 15% is also a positive development. Like any cost of doing business, taxes are simply passed on to the consuming public in the price of goods and services, and so it must be. As they go so goes the cost of living, so downward pressure on business taxes, besides boosting employment, is ultimately a benefit to all.

Liberals claim we can't afford those tax cuts, which will at least theoretically stimulate the economy, but we can afford what then Minister of Social Development Ken Dryden admitted in 2005 was an unknowably expensive universal daycare program which decidedly will not.

Tom Mulcair later added that a similar program his NDP was promoting would cost, umm, "quite a bit." Didn't Tommy Douglas once say the same thing about health care? If not he should have; it presently consumes 43% of Ontario's entire budget.

Concerned about the high cost of what was already highly subsidized tuition in this country, in 2011 the Liberals advocated giving a further $1000/year to university students. The trouble with said proposal is twofold. Firstly, a thousand bucks a year won't change anyone's education plans. Secondly, it's often the comfortably well-off who send their kids to university who will benefit from the program while the working poor, for whom a university education will remain a distant dream, foot the bill, such being the inherent problem with all universal programs.

Speaking of the poor getting poorer, Green Party leader Elizabeth May once claimed that a $30 per ton carbon levy proposed by the Tories was not high enough. It should be fifty, said she, while insisting that her party would offset the acknowledged further cost of living increases with income tax reductions, AND a means-tested subsidy, thus making the poor even more dependent on government—her government—for which they would thus be constrained to vote. Another diabolical genius in public office. How lucky can we be?

As a sop to the green gods of environmentalism, recent "Conservative" budgets have provided hundreds of millions of dollars to subsidize ethanol production as an alternative fuel source. This despite the fact ethanol's health effects are unknown, its net energy savings debatable, and the inescapable fact is that as arable land is converted to ethanol producing crops it's taken out of use in the production of other cereal crops reducing supply, exacerbating demand and again driving up everyone's cost of living. Food is for eating. Putting 6.5% of the world's grain supply in people's gas tanks while others go hungry seems a tad unethical.

And while criticizing the Tories, (and the environmental movement generally) let us not overlook their ridiculous ban on Thomas Edison's incandescent light bulb. According to one electrician "the alternative fluorescent bulbs don't give off the lumens manufacturers claim, their colour rendition is atrocious—we'll all go blind trying to read by them—and this is to say nothing of the mercury vapor that will from henceforth be polluting our landfills."

NOTE: Be it ethanol subsidies, fluorescent bulbs or the banning of DDTs in insecticides thirty years ago leading, it is estimated, to the deaths of millions by malaria, every capitulation to the green lobby means someone gets hurt. But let's look at the environmental movement as a whole for a moment.

The ground-breaking *Silent Spring* (Rachel Carson, 1962) informed that pesticides would be the death of us all; *The Population Bomb* (Paul Ehrlich, 1968) that the world's crops could not sustain its population growth and that mass starvation would ensue. Prior to the Second Coming of Al Gore these books were the Bible and the Holy Grail of the environmental movement.

In reality, technological advances have more than enabled us to feed the world, (though politics often gets in the way) and pesticides cannot be definitively shown to more than very marginally increase cancer rates. Any increase is bad, granted, but consider that the smaller yields from pesticide free crops would lead to higher food prices and increasing mortality, especially among the poor who could no longer afford what would then be the increasingly expensive, cancer fighting fruits and vegetables. That was the '60s.

In the '70s global cooling was all the rage. (Enough said.) In the '80s acid rain was leading us to an "ecological Hiroshima." In reality "all rain (even prior to industrialization) is naturally acidic" and higher pH levels (to a degree) have been shown to hasten plant growth, rather than its demise.[10]

In the '90s it was the disappearing ozone layer we don't hear about anymore since scientists determined it was largely a naturally occurring cyclical phenomena. This is not to suggest that the PCB ban that decade didn't contribute to its repair or that today's bogeyman—anthropogenic (man-made) CO_2—doesn't contribute marginally to global warming. In fact it may.

Temperatures rose moderately in the '90s with CO_2 levels indicating a possible correlation, though again we're faced with the issue of causation. Note also that in the following fifteen years temperatures flat-lined while CO_2 levels continued to rise, indicating the absence of same. Even assuming the existence of a correlation, do rising levels of CO_2 cause global warming, or does naturally occurring global warming cause increasing CO_2 to be released from our warming oceans? Climate scientist Dr. Timothy Ball in fact maintains that "temperature changes before CO_2 (levels rise or fall) in every record of any duration for any time period," indicating the latter. Assuming the validity of these findings, Gore, Suzuki and Co. appear to have it literally backwards.

But what about the melting polar ice caps? Your author was stunned when Peter Mansbridge reported in early '08 on two studies in the publication *Nature* confirming that the arctic melt of late has been the result of cyclical air flow from South America to the North Pole rather than generalized global warming. I wasn't surprised Peter could read the news. I was just amazed he could do so without blushing after all the stock he and his employer have invested in the present global warming scam, advocates of which have been caught red-handed suppressing dissent, cherry picking data and otherwise brazenly cooking the climate books.

The nitty gritty on the environment? It's not as bad as you've been led to believe. MIT atmospheric scientist Richard Lindzen: "Forests are returning in Europe and the United States. Air quality has improved. Water quality has improved (and) we grow more food on less land." There are those who would brazenly pollute our land to improve their bottom line if they could (I've seen *Erin Brockovich,* okay!) but let's not go overboard.

Recall that environmentalism was promoted by communists to tie up the west's economy in red tape, (✓) and though some environmental concerns are indeed legitimate, it's obvious on the face of it that the cause itself is overblown to the nth degree.

And who subscribed to 'the cause' as much as Elizabeth May? And who wanted to tax carbon to save the planet and drive up everyone's cost of living? Was it not he whose campaigns we're regularly supported by communist volunteers? Why did they pound the pavement for Mr. Layton and not run under the communist banner themselves? Might it be that they shared Karl Marx's conviction that socialism is the first and necessary step on the road to communism?

Indeed, and as this goes to print the socialists' bedfellows on most issues, the Liberals, are leading in the polls. Presumably they'll get around to making some concrete election promises. Allow the author to highlight some of their past ones.

In the '70s the self-proclaimed Natural Governing Party campaigned against wage and price controls before implementing (what else) wage and price controls. In the '80s they campaigned against gas tax increases before imposing even greater increases than those they'd campaigned against. In the '90s readers will recall a little promise about abolishing the GST. And then there was that one about restoring integrity to the PMO, after which they were caught brazenly pilfering the public purse to finance their election campaigns. In light of the above, the real question following their 2011 election rout is why any Canadians voted for them.

The Tories aren't the only game in town obviously, but let's be real: the Grits are corrupt; the NDP is where communists go to realize their ambitions; and the Green Party has as its base a variety of tree-hugging, man-hating, anti-American zealots.

Paul Watson, president of the Sea Shepherd Conservation Society, (on the board of which Elizabeth May sat until March of '08) defines the world's human population as the AIDS of the earth and claims it should be cut by 85%, a small percentage then being allowed to reproduce in fine eugenic fashion. Who would Paul support in an election, if he could? One time Green candidate Kevin Potvin, of course, a guy who couldn't help but express his glee when the population was reduced by a few thousand on 9/11, all of which leaves one questioning how many complete and utter delusionals are hiding in the environmental woodpile.

And Canadians have more reason to vote Tory than merely a justifiable disdain for all things liberal. Foreign policy could easily top the list.

Canada is not, popular opinion notwithstanding, a peace-keeping nation. We became a legal dominion in 1867. It's argued we became a nation in 1917 when we took Vimy Ridge in four days at a cost of almost 3600 lives. Not to diminish their deaths in the least—every one is important—but we've obviously lost comparatively few over the course of our decade in Afghanistan.

Abandoning that country before it was prepared to govern itself, which may or may not have been the case in 2011, would all but negate those deaths. Nor, though, as mentioned earlier, did anyone save the military industrial complex want this to turn into another Cyprus from which we would still be trying to extricate ourselves fifteen years hence... unless, of course, we need to be there that long to keep the Taliban... or al-Qaeda... or ISIS... or whatever comes next... from realizing their ambitions. And that's about as good a lead in as I'll get to the next issue which I'll presently try to address without pulling a fatwa down on my head.

Islam: the "religion of peace" that bloodshed follows everywhere it goes. The author will defend others' religious freedom until he draws his last breath, but he will also stand up for the truth as he understands it, and in the interests of full disclosure the religion in question should probably continue to be referred to, as it once was, as "the religion of the sword." A little history is obviously in order.

Muhammad, the prophet of Islam, was born into an Arab world where each tribe worshipped its own deity, of which there were 360. His, the Quraysh tribe, worshipped the moon god Allah, thus explaining the crescent moon found on top of every mosque and minaret on the planet. Felt called as a prophet, at Mecca he told the leaders of the other tribes to destroy their gods and make his the Supreme Being. They, of course, beholden to their deities, replied in the negative and threatened his well-being.

Fleeing north to Medina he again tried to sell himself as a prophet, this time to the Jewish and Christian communities, with the same results (minus the death threats, presumably). It is a basic tenet of the Muslim faith that he left, returned with an army and in one day beheaded between six and nine hundred Jewish leaders. *The hadiths,* the authoritative teachings and sayings of Muhammad, inform that he was the perfect example of how to live the Muslim life. And thus when you see Muslims beheading "infidels" today, they are in fact and in deed imitating their prophet. Upon his return to Mecca with 10,000 men in arms, the leaders of the other tribes saw the light and acquiesced to his earlier demands. And so it was that Islam became the dominant religion in the region: by the sword.

Surah 29:46 instructs that "Our God (the God of Islam) and your (Judeo-Christian) God is one." Now it's true that the God of the Old Testament, who according to Scripture does not change, did over the course of time order the destruction of a number of people groups, but note that it wasn't because they failed to convert to Judaism. It was because their cup of sin was overflowing, and as a holy and just God (assuming that He exists and can be described as such) He arguably had the right to do so. One must also point out, though, that there is a world of difference between a righteous God punishing people for their sin and a prophet, who claimed to have had a vision, slaying them merely for their failure to convert.

In 1891, the Viceroy of India proposed raising the age of consent in that country after an eleven-year-old wife died following sexual intercourse with her considerably more mature husband.[11] Why is this relevant? Because *the hadiths* also acknowledge Muhammad's marriage to a six year old, and according to historian Dr. Behram Moshiri no less than eleven of the prophet's thirty wives died within twenty-four hours of the consummation of their vows.

The Bible says that if one even so much as causes one of these little ones to stumble it would be better for that one if a heavy millstone were tied around his neck and he be cast into the sea. *The hadiths,* alternatively, encourage followers to imitate one who would be referred to today as a serial abuser if even only what they themselves say of him is true.

So one holy book warns against child abuse; the other encourages the imitation of one who can very reasonably be described as a prolific abuser. Muhammad claimed to serve the God of Abraham, Isaac and Jacob. In light of these contradictions, the author humbly suggests that he could hardly have been more mistaken.

None of the preceding, of course, is meant to suggest that there aren't peaceful Muslims in the world leading exemplary lives, but for those who insist on believing Islam itself to be a peaceful religion, I offer two words: Samir Kuntar. He, after serving time for bashing a four year old girl's skull against the rocks for being Jewish, was received by Palestinians as a homecoming hero. What passes for mainstream journalism in that part of the world, *Al-Jazeera,* then threw him a big, televised fiftieth birthday party.

In 1978, nineteen year old Dalal Mughrabi led a death squad that killed thirty-nine (mostly) Israelis, many of whom were children, most of whom perished on a burning bus. Does the Palestinian authority publicly decry her for having misunderstood Islam? Nay, rather they've named two high schools, two summer camps, a town square and a soccer championship after her.

In 2011, hundreds of Pakistani clerics publicly applauded the assassination of a politician with whom they disagreed. A new convert maybe, but these were studied clerics! Do they misunderstand Islam? I submit to you that they likely understand it very well, and that denial is not just a river in Egypt, but rather it's precisely where those live who continue to call the faith that inspires these homicidal maniacs, a "religion of peace."

While on the subject of Islam, another Tory strength is their attitude toward the military itself. For decades the Liberals worked to undermine the department, and given half a chance the NDP and the Greens would surely paint flowers on our museum-bound Leopard tanks. The Tories, alternatively, are rebuilding the organization. For that reason alone they deserved their coveted majority in 2011 – greedy senators and banned light bulbs notwithstanding.

On another issue, a growing chorus of writers support the decriminalization/legalization of marijuana, but some are coming around. An English newspaper that once editorially supported the same recanted upon learning of its association with the onset of schizophrenia. That very possible correlation aside, pot is a stupefying drug, countless studies confirming its negative effects on both short and long term memories – possibly the result of the shrunken amygdala and hypothalamus evident in the autopsies of regular users.

In fact, a recently concluded twenty-year British study by Professor Wayne Hall, a highly cited author and advisor to the World Health Organization, has concluded that regular users—particularly those who began smoking in their teens—experience impaired intellectual development and a heightened risk of developing psychotic disorders, and often graduate to harder drugs. Not everyone who smokes maryjane goes on to become a crack addict obviously, but if it isn't a gateway drug why did every junkie in the country start out smokin' a spliff?

In light of this, why would Liberals and socialists be so gung-ho for the decriminalization/legalization of weed? First of all, let's acknowledge that there's little difference, philosophically, between them. Let's also acknowledge that there's little difference, beyond the bayonet, between socialists and communists. And if these things are true, then frankly there's not that much light showing between liberalism and communism. (This might explain Trudeau the Lesser's admitted infatuation with China, which I thank him profusely for acknowledging.)

So all I'm saying is that if Liberals and socialists support liberalized pot laws, then it's a safe bet that Vladimir Putin does too—in the west—just like his forebears our liberalized abortion laws, the homosexual agenda and the dumbing down of our school system, etc. But why?

To answer that question, let me ask another: why did Stalin order the slaughter of more than 20,000 of Poland's finest (the officer corps and other intelligentsia) in the Katyn Forest in the spring of 1940? One theory, brought to the author's attention by Alex Debagorski of *Ice Road Truckers* fame, was that it was to dumb down the population so that they would more readily accept the communism he was preparing to shove down their throats.[12]

So I don't *know* why lefties support liberalized pot laws, but that such will over time dumb down the population—and thereby increase the likelihood of their electoral success—cannot be left unsaid. What comes after that election is the $64,000 question, but considering that Papa Trudeau uttered nary a word about patriating the constitution in the 1980 campaign, it's a safe bet you won't find it in their campaign literature.

What's that you say? The Liberals have a "scary hidden agenda?" As someone who has not been taken into their confidence I have no idea, but they sure did in 1980, and I hope you see clearly that the little surprise they foisted on us two years later has not served us well. So voting liberally, so to speak, (be that Liberal, Dipper or Green) is obviously not the answer.

Naturally the author hopes that those who vote conservatively in federal elections will do the same at the provincial level. In Alberta that increasingly obviously excludes voting PC, and the Wildrose has in many ways become just like them, leaving the newly minted Reform Party as the only refuge for my conservative-minded provincial peers.

In Saskatchewan it means voting for the Saskatchewan Party which likewise espouses a small 'c' conservative philosophy. Canada needs a "take-no-prisoners" Margaret Thatcher, granted, but every province needs a Brad Wall and Saskatchewan is lucky to have him.

Being born and raised in Manitoba, the politics of the NDP's western power base are an obvious concern. If it's something in the water, as they say, it would seem a certain member of the author's family of origin has been far too long at the well. That said, when Dad and I traveled together across vast swaths of this country from time to time it would make for great conversation and debate—and laughs—as we tried to convert each other. Politics aside where it belongs, as I alluded on the dedication page, a guy would be hard pressed to do better.

If I were still living in the province, despite the fact that they're not yet even a blip on the radar screen, I would vote for, represent or otherwise work for the Manitoba Party. Unfortunately the battle there is still largely between the NDP and the Tories, and it really doesn't matter which wins. Neither rate a second look.

Firstly, and despite their claims to the contrary, the Tories in Manitoba never balanced a budget during the Filmon years. What they did was sell off some crown corporations and incorporate that revenue, which would not be repeated, in that same year's budget – an accounting faux pas by anyone's standards. The books looked balanced, but those very temporary revenues aside government expenditures were still outstripping revenues.

To compound matters, toward the end of their term the Tories were throwing money around like drunken liberal sailors on crack, and every spending bill they put forward was (naturally) rubber stamped by the ND opposition. Under the Golden Boy that sits atop the Manitoba legislature the Tories lean left and the NDP lean right, making them all liberal, so it's time for change there, too. The Manitoba Party made a bit of a showing once. Hopefully it will again.

At the time of this writing, the Liberals are still in charge in British Columbia. That party did well by reducing the bureaucracy, balancing the budget (when they did) and privatizing some crown corporations. Good measures all.

Even what they've done, though, can be considered a small miracle considering the crippling strength of the unions in that province. The space left in this book would not be sufficient to address the problem of unions, but suffice it to say they reduce productivity, promote mediocrity and drive up everyone's cost of living. And from what feeble loins did the union movement spring forth?

I draw your attention to the year long British coal miners' strike of 1984 immortalized in the movie *Billy Elliot* (2000). Arthur Scargill headed the union. When cash got tight where did he go? Where do all kids go when they're broke? He "sought and received solace and succor from the trade unions of (then) Soviet controlled Afghanistan."[13] Except there were no trade unions in Afghanistan, which can only mean that he was collecting rubles directly from the Kremlin itself! You might not appreciate this if your dues are paid up, but he ran to daddy. And this is no baseless paternity suit.

To again quote a circular published by Stalin in 1927, part of the communist objective for the west was to "create revolt by the workers (let's call them 'strikes' for argument's sake) and intensify class war."[14] This might explain why you would find a card-carrying communist like then Alberta Federation of Labour leader Dave Werlin stirring the pot behind the picket line at the Gainers strike in '86, for but one example. The DNA tests are conclusive: the union movement is the redheaded bastard child of communism, and the NDP are soft on both, so to keep them out of office, if I lived in B.C., I'd vote Liberal. Frankly I'd vote for a bale of hay if it would keep the NDP out of office.

As Ontario's then Transportation Minister Tony Clement said to the author one day, "Ralph Klein had a burgeoning economic pie to slice up in Alberta (thanks to the price of oil and natural gas) while Mike Harris had to take essentially the same pie that previous governments had and carve it up differently to make it work." On that score the Tories did reasonably well in that province, but there's more to governing than merely bills, balance sheets and pocket books.

There are social issues to contend with, (otherwise known as life issues) and on that front they simply don't cut the mustard. In the nineties recall their penchant for subsidizing lesbian porn flicks. In the summer of '07 then Conservative boss John Tory claimed to be "delighted" to be named as a supporter of the Toronto Gay and Lesbian Film and Video Festival, showcasing such features as *The Best of Lezploitation*. And without putting too fine a point on it, let's be real: Liberal leader and present Premier Kathleen Wynne would be more likely to star in it than object to the endorsement. Frankly I'd be surprised to find more than a hair's breadth difference on most any point between the two mainline parties in the heartland, and apparently I'm not alone in that sentiment.

To quote George Jonas writing in the *National Post* after Dalton McGuinty's 2007 reelection, the residents of Ontario are just as far behind having a Liberal as opposed to a Red Tory government "implementing their equally half-baked liberal policies" – and that statement is as true today as it was the day it was first penned.

So when the mainstream parties are equally bad, what do you do? You look outside the mainstream where you find organizations like Ontario's Family Coalition Party fighting for lower and fairer taxes, responsible government and choice in education. What's that? They didn't have a candidate in your riding? Well, maybe that's because your name wasn't on the ballot.

In 2010, with economic realities punching it in the nose, Ontario reduced its budget by 2.6%. Facing the same realities, Quebec chose to increase its by 3% that year. One is mildly austere; the other profligate. Why? Transfer payments, obviously. Why tighten your belt when you can just suckle the rest of Canada for $8 billion/year according to figures published by the Canadian Taxpayers Federation?

If the author had to vote in Quebec he couldn't vote to separate because, though he may appear prone to it personally, he's morally opposed to committing economic suicide. And the threat of being drawn and quartered would not sufficiently motivate him to vote for the party of Jean Charest, a man who built his career undermining the conservative movement in this country. Fortunately he wouldn't have to vote for either following the birth of the moderately conservative Coalition Avenir Quebec in 2011.

Moving eastward, there are many people of good will and common sense in the Maritimes, but having lived there the author can tell you that there are also those who very much do subscribe to a "culture of defeat," to quote one Stephen Harper. That, of course, would be those who vote Liberal (or worse) looking for more liberal entitlements. To loosely paraphrase Alexander Fraser Tytler, (1747-1813) a democracy is doomed when its citizens realize that they can vote themselves the treasury – and that's precisely what they when voting 'liberally'. If one cares a whit for the future—that is to say, for others—they at bare minimum need to vote for fiscal responsibility.

To be sure, there is no such thing as perfect government anywhere, but contrary to popular opinion nor are they all the same. As there are people, so there are politicians who will promote injustice, there are those who will lay down beside it – and then there are those who will actively oppose it.

I draw your attention back to one William Wilburforce and the effect he had, through the machinations of British politics, on not only his native England but humanity itself. Four years into his political career, following a religious conversion he had after reading a book a travelling companion gave him, he wanted to leave politics and enter the ministry. Ex-slave ship captain, Reverend and author of the song *Amazing Grace,* John Newton, convinced him otherwise. It's a fine thing.

Between that decision and his death forty-nine years later in 1833, Wilburforce not only brought an end to slavery in the United Kingdom, but he worked tirelessly "for the alleviation of harsh child labour conditions, implemented prison reforms (and) ended the wanton use of capital punishment"[15] in the land that gave us birth. And that's besides all the Bible Society stuff.

"The Great Change," as he described it, changed Wilburforce, it changed the slave-trader Newton more than a little, and I'm confident that but for it in the author's life you would not be reading this book today. The issues contained herein would likely not motivate me as they do, and who's to say I wouldn't otherwise still be toiling away for the military somewhere?

Leaving the forces at the height of a recession in '91 was something of a step of faith, and like steps generally do it led to more of the same. And thus it was that the insurance job that followed landed me in Red Deer where I inherited the account of the ultimate good ol' boy, Kenny Hughes. Ken worked for the Canadian Taxpayers Federation, and but for his sales manager who soon thereafter became mine and assigned me to work in the area, I might have been a long time hearing of, let alone moving to, the lovely town of Barrhead where, upon the passing of John Moerman whom you will recall from the introduction, the column became a reality.

Why did I write it? Because John passed and I was there. And I figured I had it in me to do it. But why the book?

Because the truth, assuming there is some here, has to be promoted as far and wide as possible by whatever means possible. And because the columns provided what I thought was a reasonable framework on which to hang new information. I hope you agree.

But was I right to revise and update it these several times now, selling it door to door for over a decade while struggling to keep the wolf away from my own? That's a more complex question, and if you recall I was often asking it myself in the spring of '07.

One could have easily pursued a more gainful line of work. The downside to doing so, of course, is that I'd probably still have a thousand copies of that first edition in my basement. As it was, after seven years I was sharing someone else's with 3,000 copies of the fifth wondering daily if I hadn't completely gone off the rails somewhere. I suspected the fifth would be the last, but it was also about that time I drove to Winnipeg for dad's eightieth. And it was nothing if not a consequential trip.

As was not uncommon on my way across the prairies, I stopped to say 'hi' to the boys at the Taxpayers head office in Regina. This time a book in their store room caught my eye. It was on 18th century philosopher Adam Smith, and if you recall from the introduction I therein discovered that he had republished his first book, *The Theory of Moral Sentiments,* a book on social issues, (did someone say 'gay marriage') five times. (Further revisions were precluded by his death in 1790.) At any other time in my life that would have been an inconsequential piece of trivia, but coming to me when it did it literally drove me back to the drawing board for an almost complete rewrite of what would become the sixth edition.

Motivational speaker Charles "Tremendous" Jones says, "The things in your life that change you are the people you meet and the books you read," and that one did all that. It was a book about a guy who wrote a book that came into my possession at precisely the right moment to compel me to sit down and rewrite this one, one more time. Make that nine times now. I include this information to drive home the fact that Jones was right: books can influence people—and events—if they're read.

A book was instrumental, recall, in Wilburforce's conversion, ultimately impacting millions. Alexander Solzhenitsyn is credited in part with having brought down the Berlin Wall through the power of his pen. Can this little effort accomplish the author's far more modest objectives of influencing the political landscape in Canada? That, now, is going to be up to you.

If you enjoyed it, I want to encourage you to forward my web address **www.fixcanada.ca** to every Canadian in your address book where they can read an excerpt. And then buy more books. I openly admit my bias, and that I stand to benefit materially if they do, but I reckon that no less than 34,000,000 Canadians should read this one. I also calculate that you have people in your life (family, friends, neighbours, colleagues and the next person you meet walking down the street) who probably won't unless and until you put a copy in their hands.

So how do we *'Fix Canada'*? One man at a time, by changing the way people think, and frankly I know of no better way to do so than by giving them something to read. If you recall it's through reading that liberals become conservative, so it's worth a try. Of course, there are more important issues in life than political philosophy....

I've told you a bit about my journey of faith here, wrote of some stalwarts like Wilburforce and came pretty close a few times but have thus far avoided directly preaching to you. Nor will I start now. You didn't buy a political book, if you did, to get the Billy Graham treatment and I respect that.

You would agree, though, that if I had the cure for cancer and didn't tell you I would be negligent. Well, I have what I believe is something arguably more important and would in fact be very negligent if I didn't at least point you to where you could hear more.

To that end, you are invited to read my brief, thirty page autobiography at **www.jeffwillerton.com**. I'm not sure why the Pulitzer committee hasn't called yet... but it's good! One woman claims it's the funniest book she's ever read. And it's free, so enjoy.

In conclusion, allow me to say that what you hold in your hands is simply one layman's attempt at improving the political landscape in this country. It's been a labour of love, but when I finished writing the column in 1999 I figured I'd said my peace, and I think I've come to that point again. Once again I suspect this edition will be the last.

To quote Edmund Burke, "All that is required for evil to succeed is for good (people) to remain silent." So don't. Speak, write, get involved in the political process, take out a membership with the provincial and federal party of your choosing and give a little something of yourself toward the improvement of society.

In closing, God bless. May your roots always deepen and your fruit increase, and as I closed off the last column so many years ago I say again: may you prosper and be in good health as your soul prospers... and may our paths cross again soon.

Bibliography

1. *The Rescue of Capitalism: getting Adam Smith right,* Dr. James Dyce, Stress Publications, 1990, p. 21.
2. *Conflict of the Ages,* Arno C. Gaebelein, Loizeaux Brothers Inc, 1983, (Orig. 1933) p. 106.
3. Ibid, p. 72.
4. *The Social Organization of Sexuality: Sexual Practices in the United States,* E.O. Laumann et al., University of Chicago Press, 1994, p. 295.
5. Gaebelein, p. 106.
6. *Amazing Grace in the Life of William Wilburforce,* John Piper, Crossway Books, 2006, p. 31.
7. *Thomas Jefferson: The Art of Power,* Jon Meacham, Random House, 2013, p. 375.
8. *Saddam's Secrets,* Georges Sada, Integrity Publishers, 2006.
9. *The Trouble with Canada... Still,* William D. Gairdner, BPS Books, 2010.
10. *The Skeptical Environmentalist: Measuring the Real State of the World,* Bjorn Lomberg, Cambridge University Press, 2001, p. 178.
11. *The Decline and Fall of the British Empire,* Piers Brendon, Vintage Books, 2008, p. 238.
12. *King of the Road, True Tales from a Legendary Ice Road Trucker,* Alex Debagorski, the Penguin Group, 2010, p. 9.
13. *The Downing Street Years,* Margaret Thatcher, Harper Collins Publishers, 1993, p. 369.
14. Gaebelein, p. 106.
15. Piper, pp. 41,2.

To order more copies of
FIX CANADA
call 1.877.601.0708